AN AUSABLE READER

A Decade of Poetry Against the Current
1999—2008

Edited by Chase Twichell

AUSABLE PRESS
2008

Cover art: Painting of the Ausable River
"Butterfly Rock" by Paul Matthews, 2001. Acrylic on board, 20 x 18"

Design and composition by Ausable Press
The type is Jenson with Trajan Titling.
Cover design by Rebecca Soderholm

Published by
AUSABLE PRESS
1026 HURRICANE ROAD
KEENE, NY 12942

Distributed to the trade by
CONSORTIUM BOOK SALES & DISTRIBUTION
34 THIRTEENTH AVENUE NE, SUITE 101
MINNEAPOLIS, MN 55413-1007
(612) 746-2600
Order FAX: (800) 351-5073
Orders: (800) 283-3572
Individual orders: www.coppercanyonpress.org

All works reprinted with the permission of the authors.
For author photo credits, see page 312.

Library of Congress Cataloging-in-Publication Data
An Ausable reader : a decade of poetry against the current, 1999–2008
edited by Chase Twichell.–1st ed.
p. cm.
ISBN 978-1-931337-45-8 (alk. paper)
1. American poetry—21st century. 2. American poetry—20th century.
I. Twichell, Chase, 1950— II. Ausable Press.

PS617.A94 2008
811'.608--dc22
2008047723

AN AUSABLE READER

A BRIEF HISTORY OF AUSABLE PRESS
A Letter from the Editor

When I started Ausable Press in 1999, I had in mind a new model for publishing—a fusion of the old letterpress aesthetic, which was my background, with the seemingly vast potential of computers and the internet. It had become possible for a single person to start a small business from scratch with a fraction of the capital it would have required only a decade before. I set out to learn the new technology and the intricacies of the business with the help and encouragement of many people. I'm especially grateful to Dan and Jeanne Halpern of Ecco Press for their generosity and advice, and to Barry Moser of Pennyroyal Press for teaching me everything I know about design.

At the time, the venerable old commercial houses still ruled the world of poetry publishing, although a number of independent literary presses like City Lights, Copper Canyon, Graywolf, BOA and Sarabande were well established, and many university presses still considered the publishing of poetry a part of their mission. In the last decade, the geography has shifted dramatically. The opportunities for poets have steadily diminished, with many commercial houses and university presses curtailing their lists or even closing them entirely. Funders of independent presses such as the National Endowment for the Arts and state arts councils have had their budgets cut drastically. The situation has become especially dire for new poets and for those in mid-career.

It quickly became obvious that there was a real need for presses like Ausable. The first year, we received 1,200 unsolicited manuscripts (thereafter, an average of 800 per year). I made a commitment to run the Press for ten years, with the objective of building a viable business that could then be passed on to a larger institution. What began as a one-person enterprise quickly evolved into a not-for-profit corporation with boards of directors and advisory editors, five employees (all of whom worked for far less than their time was worth), expanded office space, a web site and e-store, and annual catalog.

Ausable's mission has been "to publish poetry that investigates and expresses human consciousness in language that goes where prose cannot. We believe that art is our best hope of understanding our world, and that poetry in particular has the power to change the way we perceive ourselves in that world. We also believe that independent presses have a responsibility to nurture and preserve for future generations our clearest thinking and expression, especially in this age of war and ecological gambling."

Our authors include a Poet Laureate, National Book Award, National Book Critics Circle Award, and Pulitzer Prize-winners, new poets, and poets in mid-career whose work deserves greater recognition. In the last decade we've published thirty-eight books by thirty-one authors.

Several years ago, I approached Copper Canyon Press in Port Townsend, Washington, the largest independent publisher of poetry in the United States, about the possibility of adding Ausable to their list. They were excited by the idea, and in January 2009, Ausable Press officially became part of Copper Canyon. We couldn't be happier with the marriage. There is a deep compatibility of taste and aesthetics, and a shared passion for poetry. In Copper Canyon, Ausable has found the ideal home. —Chase Twichell

A Note from the Editor of Copper Canyon Press

Copper Canyon Press was founded in 1972 and continues publishing today in the belief that poetry is vital to language and living. Throughout our history Copper Canyon has sought to support poets at every stage of their lives and art. The Press's list of books includes major award-winning poets alongside some of the most exciting younger poets, important works in translation from the great poetries of the world, and out-of-print classics.

When Chase Twichell approached me about the possibility of Copper Canyon Press caretaking the books she had published via Ausable, I enthusiastically embraced the possibility. In less than a decade Chase and her colleagues on Ausable's staff and board have built one of the most respected poetry lists in America and one of the most professional of independent presses on the scene. Copper Canyon's commitment to the independent publishing spirit and its tradition of well-made, well-edited books, alongside Ausable's similar attention to design as well as its impeccable editorial vision made this a union we couldn't resist.

As non-profit organizations, both Copper Canyon and Ausable were born out of an independent do-it-yourself sensibility and have thrived—sometimes against all logic—during a period wherein the larger publishing industry has been increasingly volatile and answerable to multinational shareholders. During Ausable's lifetime, the growth of international media conglomerations and the blossoming of big-box bookstores, have left a wake of independent bookstore closures, overblown author advances, and out-of-print books. The challenge of printing literary titles has grown ever more daunting and small publishing operations have become increasingly difficult to sustain. As the past thirty-five years have shown us, Copper

Canyon, Ausable and other non-profits cannot continue their programs without the support of donors, and readers who share in our belief in the importance of poetry and books. It has been such support which has made the Ausable-Copper Canyon union possible. In years to come we look forward to sharing new books by many of the same authors included in this anthology, but for now we hope you'll enjoy the poems gathered here and perhaps buy a book or two by their authors. —*Michael Wiegers*

JONATHAN AARON
Journey To the Lost City (2006)

Jonathan Aaron is the author of two previous collections of poetry. His work has received many honors, including Fellowships from Yaddo, McDowell, and the Massachusetts Endowment for the Arts. His poems, essays, and reviews have been widely published in periodicals including *The Paris Review, The New York Review of Books,* and *The Times Literary Supplement.* His poems have appeared in *Best American Poetry* five times. Aaron lives in Cambridge, Massachusetts and teaches at Emerson College.

In his own words: "A poem should show you—visually—something you haven't really seen or looked at before. It should do something surprising, loudly or quietly, with language. It should also at some level question any pattern it seems attracted to or ready to settle for. I would like my poems to range in any way they wish between the regions of prose on the one hand and the regions of incantation on the other."

THIS LITTLE SYSTEM

of branchy twigs a few dead leaves
still cling to, along with three or four
shreds of sun-stiffened paper, a bit of string,
occasionally a weather-faded ribbon, feels

prickly, oddly solid, yet ready to float
from your hand. Lidded—roofed—it might be
a box or a tiny house meant for nothing
bigger than a bird or a mouse. Don't ask me

why at night it emits a fitful glow,
abrupt flashes, periodic spokes of light.
What do I know? Someone inside's up late

reading, or snooping with a flashlight. Or signalling
that long, low, darkened ship lying in
close to shore, doubtless up to no good.

THE END OF *OUT OF THE PAST*

(RKO Pictures, 1947)

"I never told you I was anything but what I am," she says.
Black and white, the sunset behind Lake Tahoe looks spectacular.
She turns and goes upstairs, his chance to light a cigarette
and dial the operator. She slips the pistol into her briefcase,
gives the bathroom a cursory final glance. Moments later,
sitting on the couch, he hands her a shot of brandy.
"Thanks," she says. "Por nada," he answers, pouring one
for himself. She says she thinks they both deserve a break. "We deserve
each other," he replies, and wings his glass into the empty fireplace.
She's unperturbed, strictly business, already in Mexico.
His sleepy expression shows he knows exactly where they're going.
Night has already covered most of the country. The airwaves
are vibrating with the strains of "Sentimental Journey," "Satin Doll,"
and "String of Pearls." As they get into his Chevy station wagon,
I could be five and just waking up from another nightmare.
Half the world is lying in ruins.

SKILLS

Blondin made a fortune walking back and forth
over Niagara Falls on a tightrope—blindfolded,
or inside a sack, or pushing a wheelbarrow, or perched on stilts,
or lugging a man on his back. Once, halfway across,
he sat down to cook and eat an omelette.

Houdini, dumped into Lake Michigan chained
and locked in a weighted trunk, swam back to the boat
a few moments later. He could swallow more than a hundred needles
and some thread, then pull from between his lips
the needles dangling at even intervals.

I can close my eyes and see your house
explode in a brilliant flash, silently,
with a complete absence of vibration. And when I open them again,
my heart in my mouth, everything is standing
just as before, but not as if nothing had happened.

THE WOLF OF GUBBIO

for Anthony Hecht

It was one of those towns with practically no perspective,
the architecture half-geometrical, houses upon houses
stacked at dizzy angles. Clouds the shape and color of laurel leaves
hung in a pale blue sky. The locals walking around wore
guilty looks, conscious, as always, of having something to hide.
Flowers grew in doorways, abundant, untended, extending
themselves in gestures of inquiry and yearning. Iridescent songbirds
plunged through the air, heedless of what might be waiting
in the forest at the foot of mountains that appeared
deliberately jagged. An angel, robed and golden-haired,
floated absent-mindedly above a garden. Farther off
and smaller in scale, a bat-winged devil, whose grimace
augured either laughter or tears, crouched on a rooftop.
A lake, or possibly the sea, gleamed at the distant end of a road
that wound through other towns, each a staid collection of arches
and towers like bunches of white asparagus in the noonday sun.
Saint Francis liked to sing in French and knew the troubadors.
Bending forward, he did not look directly into the eyes of the animal,
who cocked his head, thought for a moment, and started wagging his tail.

LOOKING AT ROUSSEAU'S
SLEEPING GYPSY

for Anna

A gypsy girl decides to visit her grandmother
on the other side of the desert. Carrying a staff,
a jar of water to quench her thirst, and a lute for music
to keep her company, she travels all day.
It's getting dark when she arrives at an oasis.
After she eats a few dates and drinks some water,
she picks up her lute and sings herself a song.
Then she lies down and quickly falls asleep.
She doesn't see the moon rise, and the stars as well,
and the night turn into an approaching lion.
Lions eat anything from insects to antelopes and giraffes.
This one has to be at least ten feet long from the end of his tail
to the tip of his nose. I can't tell you what he's doing here.
I don't know why he's not back home in some African savannah.
He walks up to the sleeping girl. Maybe she's dreaming about
her grandmother, whom she counts on seeing tomorrow. Maybe not.
The desert is completely silent, except for a jackal barking
faintly and far off. The lion looks around with a shining eye,
and a breeze stirs his yellow mane as it would the curtain
across the window the girl sleeps next to in really hot weather.
No, I don't think the lion is going to eat her. Yes,
you could say she's wearing a brand new dress.

ANXIOUS DREAMS

How lucky I am tonight to be holding a lantern
at this railroad crossing in the middle of America
and not clinging to a leaky raft on the north Atlantic,
or plunging from a cliff in Nepal because my rope broke.
As the lights and noise of the train wane and die out,

I can hear my wife snoring into her pillow
and the dogs on either side of our bed snoring
into theirs. What was it I was doing a moment ago?
That's it: trying to remember the name of the actor
who played the Lone Ranger on the radio.

The Lone Ranger on the radio always sounded as if he had a cold.
Clayton Moore played the role on television. I hope Clayton
Moore and Jay Silverheels as Tonto, the Lone Ranger's faithful
Indian companion, were friends in real life. Or at least
that they more than just respected each other.

Whoa, there. Steady, big fellow, the masked man would say
reassuringly to his horse Silver, who spooked sometimes,
then always calmed at the sound of his master's voice…
A sudden beam of light through a hole in the clouds
silhouettes a hovering bird of prey. It occurs to me

that Tonto's hardy pinto and Silver are like
Gunnar Björnstrand's squire and Max Von Sydow's knight
in Bergman's early film, *The Seventh Seal.*
I'm in the middle of the fourteenth-century,
having just stepped onto Swedish soil

after twenty wasted years in the Holy Land.
Soon a third of Europe's population will die of the Plague.
Our crusade was so stupid, the squire tells me,
that only an idealist could have thought of it.
The knight is staring intently at the palm of his hand,

his pulse quickening at the prospect of playing chess
with Death. One moment I'm standing beside them,
the next I'm all alone on the crest of a steep dune
overlooking the Baltic. Far below, two horses
are walking fetlock-deep in the foaming shallows.

Knight and squire lie motionless on the sand, where hunger
and exhaustion must have dropped them into anxious dreams.
Two more horses amble into view, a white Arabian followed by
a stocky paint. The four of them touch noses, nod to each other,
and lower their heads to the nervous, undrinkable water.

NIGHT OF THE DEMON

(Columbia Pictures, 1957)

A strip of paper with words on it
in a dead language jerks from your fingers
as if tied to an invisible string.
It scampers straight into the fire, then
up the chimney in a single ash. And suddenly
who you were isn't who you are.

Yesterday, your god was the scientific method.
Now, you don't have time to even laugh
at anyone who thinks this world is still the one in which
not far from here a tired farmer stables his horses
for the night, children ponder their schoolwork,
a woman dials her sister in Lyme Regis.

Driving too fast through the hopeless dark,
the trees and hedgerows blurred
in their frantic rush away from your destination,
all you can see in your headlights' sickening glare
is that momentary feather of flame,
and the ghost of your own hand grasping at nothing.

OFFERING

for J.B.

Some evening, after I've been dead a few years,
when the cabs are busy sideswiping each other in the rain,
just as they're doing right now (a few things won't have changed
that much), maybe I'll be the sensation of a cool hand
on your forehead as you drive across what's left of the Brooklyn Bridge
into Manhattan and look up, suddenly not yourself, at the tall
black monuments stacked this way and that in the sulphurous air.
Or maybe I'll be the radio glow's low-volume sibilance of words
and music you've been hearing but not really listening to, or the surmise
starting to come to you as you take a right onto 6th Avenue, a moment
of silence in the storm carrying headlong more or less everybody
toward the latest spectacles of love and corruption. And yet, and yet—
later that night, for one reason or another maybe you'll think of me
and spill a few willy-nilly drops from your shot of Bushmills onto the floor
in memory of my first steps into eternity.

JULIE AGOOS
Property (2008)

Julie Agoos is the author of two previous collections of poetry, *Above the Land* (Yale University Press, 1987) and *Calendar Year* (Sheep Meadow Press, 1996). For eight years a Lecturer in the Creative Writing Program at Princeton University, she is now a Professor of English and Coordinator of the MFA Program in Poetry at Brooklyn College/CUNY, where she has taught since 1994. She lives in Nyack, New York.

In her own words: "I'm interested in poems interacting with and infiltrating each other. 'One perception moving instanter on another' was Olson's take on poetic form, but for me poems are both quick and slow—forward-moving energy and resistance to movement—utterance, but also a kind of listening. I love those tensions, and the rhythmic intervals between words and lines in the ear, and poem to poem in a book. *Property* is many voices telling stories; I worked to capture the movement from one voice and tone to another, and to create an effect of both layering and unearthing; of History pressing against the individual human voice."

FRONTIER

On the road you passed a house done up in paint—
a billboard, a hideout. Expecting fire,
a spray of bullets from upstairs, you read:
DIE YELLOW DOG—the stars and stripes
were there of course, beneath a sky of black.
The paint had been thickly applied, then spread
with a broom or cloth, and then inscribed.
Along the bottom edge a child had added
one yellow sun, a fence, some tulips
to a meadow full of green grass
that mixed right into the yellow brush
so that you couldn't tell for once where nature ended.

PRIMOGENITURE

Someone put that basket under the dresser.
Chose to. Bent. Kicked it maybe.
Not the first time, it's spent
years there, unthought of; only some time out
of exile chasing a life
in the sun. The blond wood is well-stained
for all that. It has held sandwiches, beer, a knife,
sunscreen and clippers. Diapers. Once,
a specimen of toadstool that ate that hole
right through the end. But it was strong enough!
I remember it full of gloves and a Peterson's Guide,
peonies roughly shoved through the upright handles.
And her hand pulling the weight, and the shadow it cast
on the terrace—like a sundial—
a penny from the war lay in the fretwork,
I remember that, working its way in or out—
and, lifting it from her, the light
weight that made my hand feel light.
That's just as clear today as when
she came in from the garden late
and put that burden down right here.

PROPERTY

They used to call him the Indian.
Because he was tall and sunburned, and
because you could not look him in the eyes.
He used to do yardwork, that's hard labor
when you get right down to it, in rocky soil
and so far north. He had a plan. Eradicated
every noxious plant for miles;
and because of his inhuman strength,
he was irreplaceable. That meant
he belonged to each one
who employed him. He was that gifted.
He unnerved them when he said:
"I am but the first slave on my farm."

READING OF LEBANON

The street now no entry,
and tapered by rubble;
the sidewalk unpacked,
the schoolyard all inventory,

500 chairs in the sun
and miles of linoleum flooring
flecked by mortar; 500
polished desks in open air.

3 o'clock:
eclipse of bells. A glitter
of chalk through the hi-tech
network (wherever

legible) of window
or door—
still framing the skeletal
abstract of classroom and hall.

Oh, Strict and Familiar Mother
of Seasons: such light
scores the board
with the ropes to be learned in the ceasefire there

between three and dinner!

PASTORAL

The moon on time last night above the hill—
first a corrola of light, giving the outlines
of steeple, grange, and firehouse and school.
Then the eyes, as it were, peering over the crest,
and the lake picking up light, the sky a clamor
of bats, moths, squirrels—the quiet ones—
such that I said to my daughter: Imagine
when men didn't know the cause
of the moon's fast rising in the dark, on fire!
What fear you'd have felt! And my child said:
"But I don't know why and I do feel fear."

HINDSIGHT

"I had known him as a child
when he played guitar: thin,
hyperactive; with a clear soprano then.

Later, the golden curls had straightened
and grown dark. He played nothing now
but of a doubt so broad his family feared for him:

talent like that drives the nails in, they said,
although it was the world he hammered out,
as when he entered me it seemed the source

of all knowledge had been displaced. More curse
than song. More freedom from remorse in him
that longed to give up self-love to desire,

but meant: to have been bound by nothing, like a photograph;
the black and white of him his skill protected
a mood more fundamental than the song itself.

While my one art, for which he'd blame me still,
despite the years it's taken to uncomplicate
that touch of his, which had reviled flesh

so fully as it took the place of music,
is that I've never known how to forget
that history of his: how Song

once followed him, rained down
and filled him from a high cloud: knowledge
like a cleaving; amnesty I would not grant."

LET US STRIVE ON TO FINISH THE WORK WE ARE IN

The past is so *clean*, seen
from the hill in the perfect aftermath
of your telling me. Between
those facts and this likeness
which can both be reached
by rail, by bus, by car,
between that passionate field
and the photo in the guidebook, this
faith, unstoried,
one wears on one's sleeve
like a star; this guilt
that one did not play a part.
When the Law stepped in to say,
it's legend now, I breathed
a sigh of relief
—it was all so long ago—
and closed the book
on someone else's life. But look: now
it is as if that summer returned,
and we went in one by one to bathe,
very far up the tremendous stairs.

OVERNIGHT

All the familiar contours chasten.
The lake is a pool of dark thought.
There, the clouds bear pale change,
gathered in contemplation.

The lake is a cup of gray fear:
your body in the cold dawn
upturned, and my own drowning eye
opened on the floating light.

And I can see the pines unclasp
each from each, and the sky
rising a little, and always the world
under its leaf of gold.

And I can hear the black ice take
around the island's certainty,
and my own voice, and a pair
of loons unmooring in the mind's ear.

PAMELA ALEXANDER
Slow Fire (2007)

Pamela Alexander is the author of three previous collections: *Inland, Commonwealth of Wings,* and *Navigable Waterways,* a Yale Younger Poets selection. After teaching for many years at the Massachusetts Institute of Technology, she joined the faculty of Oberlin College where she is associate editor of *Field* magazine. An active outdoors-woman, Alexander often finds the beginnings of poems as she bikes, hikes, kayaks, and cross-country skis.

In her own words: "My poems usually start with bits of language. A phrase sounds urgent or strange or musical; once I write it down it attracts other bits of language, like a molecule building itself. The phrase may come from something visual that I consciously turn into words or from some detail of natural history I've read (the size of an owl's brain, say, or the names of ferns. Often I don't know where it came from. I work in a notebook until I have a sense of where the cluster of lines is going, and then I revise (and revise and revise) on a computer. Often poems begin when I'm outdoors, enjoying myself in a kayak or on a trail, when I think I'm not thinking about writing at all."

LETTER HOME

I can't write you because everything's
wrong. Before dawn, crows swim
from the cedars: black coffee calls them down,
its bitter taste in my throat as they circle,
raucous, huge. Questions with no
place to land, they cruise yellow air
above crickets snapping
like struck matches. My house on fire, crows

are the smoke. You've never left me.
When you crossed the river you did not
call my name. I stood in tall grass
a long time, listening to birds
hidden in reeds, their intricate songs.

The grass will burn, the wrens,
the river and the rain that falls on it.
I can go nowhere else: everything
I cannot bear is here.

I must listen deeper. Sharpen my knife.
Something has changed the angles
of trees, their color. Do not wait to hear
from me. I cannot write to you
because this is what I will say.

HERE WE ARE

Today it is. Right here next to
yesterday which, wanting

to be perfect, fell down. Today's
morning opens big doors

but doesn't know what to do
with itself. It has a chair and a hill

and a window between. It can look out
and in. Nothing sits in the chair, nothing

moves on the hill. Beyond the hill
is a darker hill, but today hasn't

gotten that far.
                    I am around here
somewhere. Today tries the chair,

stands at the window. It stands
on the hill, too, talking to itself

with the sound of daylight.
It stops wondering what

to do: it has half a planet to get to
and the half keeps moving. It has

to make hay, it has to make trees.
I am a here. A standing. I hold

sky in my hands, which are empty,
which have let slide the economy

of clocks. Now is an economy
of air. It has abundance but is not

full. It stands around me. I stand
around it. Now it is.

FROM THE BASTIDE

the walled town of Puycelsi, Midi-Pyrénées

Stone village brightened by wooden shutters
painted blue. The glass opens inward,
lace panels swaying.

Yesterday, at dawn, a small bat flew inside to rest.

I often talk to the past as if to a child, hoping
it will learn. Now I must talk to the present also
because it happens in two languages.

I am a stranger. Where is the post office? The store?
What color is the sky in this country?

Narrow streets. Lean past lace, past blue, take
a peach from the facing neighbor's table.

The bat

As I think again of the bat, write *The bat*,
the bat flies in. Audible landing.
It crawls behind the bureau, clings.

Songs in the square at night. Beyond the walls,
stars. Owls. Lyrics mostly in English.

Dear C, You are not interested in being with someone. You
are interested in the appearance of being with someone.

There is no bread here on Mondays.

//

The men at the bar have sheep shit and straw
stuck to their boots. They are drinking beer
against the sound of rain at ten in the morning.

The dog lies on the stone floor, ears up,
alert idiom. He calls himself Idiot.

The store is not open much. The post office
less. (Dear C, You are pond scum—)
Village so small it's all edge, far above fields
white with mist at dawn.

By noon some of the mist has stayed
as sheep. Other fields dissolve to
sunflowers: crop and ornament.

Foreigner, she leaves the fruit and eats the plate.

Now there is an argument in the bar, everyone
vehement. Good to be "English," ignored.
Don't want to go outside; the rain would notice me.

Foreigner, she ate a horse.

Dear C, You are an artist all right.
Reading in bed: the book opens the window. When she
falls asleep, the window closes.

//

The words line up, ready;
no moment surprises. I load phrases,
a future pretending to be the present.

Otherwise.

Have you seen the button from my wolf? I have lost him.

Yesterday a white day, no shadows. We wandered,
counting waterfalls and losing count. Butterflies
in zones as we climbed. Black at first; in the high meadows,
yellow, or pale blue with white edges. Fewer
at the rocky summit, and all white.

Back late. A stone on the doorstep
turns into a toad. Sparkling
wine and cous-cous

and the town loud with tinsel music
from a little fair. Its carousel
crowded with spaceships, motorcycles,
tanks with guns. Just one paltry dragon
and something like a llama.

Sixty-year-olds dance
under strings of colored lights.
The music follows us home, upstairs, to bed.

//

The bar's window looks to a slant of hill. Some clouds
drift left to right, like reading, so I see them first.
Some clouds go the other way.

The clock strikes twice each hour. It just struck twelve.
In a few minutes it will be noon again.

Oh, Mother, You should have seen the butterflies!
Different colors for different altitudes, like signage
—a good thing, since the trails weren't otherwise
marked. My pack was green, his orange: perhaps
the butterflies read us too. Dear C, Months ago you asked if
you were my first foreign lover. Did you think I
told the truth? You certainly didn't. You're an artist all right—

Dear Anne, It's raining cats and dogs, and one of the dogs
has come in and is lying on the stone floor
like a smart dog, even though his name
is Idiot. Red wine, wet dog smell—

—a con artist. May you
get what you want, the appearance
of love. May you—

Postcard to myself. Dear X, Remember
that the blue paint on the shutters is sticky
and takes your fingerprints,
that owls make the dogs bark,
that so much light and coffee make you dizzy.

Remember to be polite.
Remember not to eat the table, exactly.

You will find your way, you know, or
you will make it.

May we all get more than we
can think to want.

Yes. I would like to rain.

ROUND

Boats we are. The light
we float on rises, ebbs.

Weather is water

and its ways. It's where
we live, big
blue planet

in our heads. Light
washes in.

Out. The life
we float on. Boats.

KEITH ALTHAUS
Ladder of Hours (2005)

Keith Althaus is the author of *Rival Heavens* (Provincetown Arts Press, 1993). His poems have appeared in *Virginia Quarterly Review, American Poetry Review, The New Yorker,* and numerous other magazines and journals. He has worked at many jobs, including loft renovation, tree planting, carpentry, and clerical work, and now runs a gallery with his wife, the painter Susan Baker. They live in North Truro, Massachusetts.

In his own words: "While technically these poems cover many years, more than half my life, it is in fact no time: the pleasures and sorrows that preoccupied me when I began have not gone away, but have grown clearer, sharper, more insistent upon being heard. And the mysteries I set out to explore have, as mysteries do, only deepened and widened. I stand no nearer conclusion now than I did then, yet, as if in compensation, writing has given me a second, concurrent life, more like a companion than a shadow.

A poet can only hope his wild stabs occasionally strike bone, a startling occurrence for both the reader and writer. It's fitting for an art born of solitude that we share these moments alone."

LITTLE ELEGY

Even the stars wear out.
Their great engines fail.
The unapproachable roar
and heat subside
as wind blows across
the hole in the sky
with a noise like a boy
playing on an empty bottle.
It is an owl, or a train.
You hear it underground.
Where the worms live
that can be cut in half
and start over
again and again.
Their heart must be
in two places at once, like mine.

HOMECOMING

We drove through the gates
into a maze of little roads,
with speed bumps now,
that circled a pavilion,
field house, and ran past
the playing fields and wound
their way up to the cluster
of wood and stone buildings
of the school you went to once.
The green was returning to
the trees and lawn, the lake
was still half-lidded with ice
and blind in the middle.
There was nobody around
except a few cars in front
of the administration. It must
have been spring break.
We left without ever getting out
of the car. You were quiet
that night, the next day,
the way after heavy rain
that the earth cannot absorb,
the water lies in pools
in unexpected places for days
until it disappears.

POEM

I felt nothing
driving by your city,
no magnet tug
greater than any other,
just old water tanks,
oil reserves, malls
and miles of fast-food restaurants
and struggling store fronts
pulling for a different
reason; none of it
has any hold on me,
but looking down
those long streets
of little houses,
with trees grown up,
the driveways overflowing,
and the shining acres of cars
bowing down before
a single god, I didn't
hear one heartbeat
above the motor,
or words like music
caught in the hollows
of a swing set,
or any other place
the air stagnates:
a box with grass
and water, stars
punched in the top
so we can breathe.

REVOLUTION IN THE AIR

Reading how this party split
into two factions, one of which
survived into the '90's, the other
dissolved almost immediately
over disagreements as to whether
to concentrate on cadre-building
or developing alliances within
the working-class . . .
I had to keep one finger
in the back, in the glossary,
to keep track of who's who,
and remind myself these acronyms
had faces, marched on sunny days,
in rain and wind, argued
endlessly the course of events
that never came but flowed away
from them on a tide of breaths
propelled by heartbeats, little oars
that move us closer, through
narrowing passageways,
to the future's source.

TREASURE ISLAND

for my son

Beside me
on the couch,
finally quiet
after running all day;
his knees stick out
like a pair of bruised peaches.

The room is bright,
a box of light
floating in darkness.
Windows on three sides open
so it's almost out-of-doors.
The noise of the swamp
drifts in: peepers,
and unknown wings
flapping, shaking loose,
bugs bouncing off screens,
the corners murmuring.

Although he can read now,
he'd rather listen,
like getting a ride
and watching the trudging
miles go by.
What does he see
as I read the description
of the bluff above the cove

where the pirate ship
lay anchored?
A hill nearby
where Truro
curves around the bay?
And he's Jack Hawkins I'm sure,
but who's the Squire, the Doctor,
and Long John Silver?

Citronella circulates
its smell from childhood,
now mimicking hashish,
and the lighthouse
from a mile off
casts its weak strobe
over land, together conjuring
another treasure hunt,
begun before you've got
an idea what you're
looking for, only
what it is not.
Behind the laced sugar water
taste the metal of the spoon,
like blood, and hear again
the heroic music turning tinny,
as everything slows
like a film caught until
it burns in front of
the projector's naked bulb,
a light behind the eyes
that won't go out.

That time is kept alive
like a match cupped
against the wind, a candle
in a skull, flickering tonight
in uneven breaths,
as sleep,
the dark sub-text,
the undertow
in the story-teller's voice
pulls him under, and carries
him off to an island
overgrown with the vegetation
of dreams and peopled
by composites
from the day's dismemberment
by clock hands. `

Then, subtly altered, its mass
magnetized, his head
is charged with dreams,
and leaning next to mine
generates their waking
counterpart: wishes,
but all in the negative:
may he avoid this,
be spared that,
not have to go through
something else . . . the list
cuts out a silhouette, faceless,
blind with bliss,
while I revisit another night,

an afternoon stretched into evening
in a dealer's pad on Eleventh Street,
across the table from Bobby Driscoll,
who, someone told me later,
"played the kid in *Treasure Island.*"

Even the small town paper
I was reading a few years later
carried the wire service obituary,
an overdose:
a clear proof of something
still unclear.
That night
when his connection came
he broke off talking
and tied his ascot
around his arm
and hunted for a vein,
then leaned back, eyes filled
with appreciation, overwhelmed
as soundless applause
spanned the living pain
separating the same person
years apart.

The dark is lined with fur,
fins, and feathers
rustling and fluttering,
their sudden silence
a trip wire across the lawn
leading to the swamp

where the tireless lighthouse
flashes its ambiguous message:
equal parts safety and danger,
and its strobe shows
the night at work:
its jumping eyes, and vines
of climbable shadows,
and interlocking circles
like magician's rings
spreading across the water
as rain brings music,
changing tempos, slowing, adding
a thousand strings
in all directions: so many
leaves struck, grasses bent,
and branches glazed.
He stirs at its cold scent;
a shiver runs through him,
then me. It's late.
I mark our place.

CRAIG ARNOLD
Made Flesh (2008)

Craig Arnold is the author of *Shells*, a Yale Younger Poets selection chosen by W.S. Merwin. A former winner of the Amy Lowell Travelling Scholarship and the Rome Prize, he was recently awarded a Fulbright to Colombia and a US-Japan Creative Artists Exchange Fellowship. He teaches in the MFA Program at the University of Wyoming.

In his own words: "As a child I was fascinated with mythology— Robert Graves, Homer, Ovid and the *Edda*. Later I fell under the spell of Eliot's *The Waste Land*, its intermingling of the eternal with the everyday and even the sordid. Most recently I came to admire the graphic novels of Neil Gaiman, rediscovering in them the child's enchantment in an old story newly told. *Made Flesh* is among other things a tip of the cap to him, his generosity and irreverence, the permission he gives his characters to shed their stiff costumes and speak the language of the street. Myth can easily degenerate into archaeology, a catalogue of ruins, an advertisement for the poet's erudition. But in the end we return to the old stories because they cut us closest to the bone, teaching us how to lose ourselves twice over—once to love, once to death."

HYMN TO PERSEPHONE

Help me remember this   how once the dead were locked
out of the ground   and wandered sleepless and sun-blinded
She was the one who took them each by the hand   helped them
lay their bodies back in the dark sweet decay
gladly   as onto a lover's bed   they call her Koré
the Maiden   a dark queen with a crown of blood-colored poppies
her fingers lift the cool coins from a dead girl's eyelids
her breath in a man's mouth releases him from memory

There was a man who would play fast and loose with Love
She smiled at first to hear him tossing around her nicknames
like cheap wedding confetti   Pretty Butt   Manslayer   Smile-lover
or mocking the blessed valentine folded up in her lap
petal-pink as a seashell   but when he swore he'd never
let Love knock the wind out of him   and leave him panting
that set her teeth on edge   Love is a cruel justice
she makes us pay for our lover's sins as well as our own
and she took away the one whose loss would hurt him deepest

Maybe he would have wept   but grim determination
came to him more easily than tears   and so he followed
the road that only the desperate walk with their eyes open
where the willows bend to comb their fingers through the river
and the long grass cuts the ankles   stalks of mullein
stand like tall candles   the dead mixed with the living
and spiders weave webs between them   glint in the sunlight
the vague gray country where all shadows gather
and the dark queen keeps them safe in her lightless mansion

She was sitting out on her porch   peeling a pomegranate
leaning back in her chair   feet propped on the railing
her face a cool and cloudless moon   ink-black hair
Who are you she called   most of my visitors come here
with their arms crossed and pennies laid over their eyes
My eyes are open he answered   nothing I do can close them
night after night I lie awake   counting my heartbeats
my hands won't work   they can't seem to hold anything

Come in the house then   she held the door half-open
and deep in the dark hallway he thought he could see the faintest
flutter of movement   and he was afraid   She took his hand
her fingers cool as a cave of water-hollowed limestone
Someone you knew she asked   this graceful tender of shadows
My advice to you is to go home and grieve her
Sound the well of your tears as deeply as you can
wipe your eyes   and be glad you're still among the living

Why he demanded   you could bring her back in a heartbeat
Maybe she said   do you think you're the first to come here
chasing after someone they lost   but you have the guilty
look of a man who tossed away what he loved too lightly
How can I feel sorry for you   You don't know the first
thing about my love he snapped   So prove it she said
sing me a love song   who is this girl you miss so much
that you come to my house to fetch her out of the shadows

44

He sang of the first permission of flesh and flesh to entangle
how we abandon the guard of our heart   and throw our borders
open   and welcome a sweet invader to take possession
the sudden exquisite catch in a throat   and the slow hush
of a breath unfettered   the sweetest sounds to a lover's ear
He sang of hands finding   shyly at first   their way
to another shelf of hips   oh how the heart flares
and melts like wax spilling over a candle's lip

Even the spiders stopped spinning their webs to listen
I like your song she said   maybe you'll come back
and sing it again for me before too long   he shivered
Out of her lawn she plucked a withered stem of mullein
Take this and go home   and you'll find her waiting
I'll give you one more day and night and the morning after
to spend together however you please   I warn you though
when the time comes   say your goodbyes   and don't look back

That day the cherry-trees in the square had just flowered
making a roof of white blossom over their heads
That day they walked   with the awkwardness of the long parted
and sat on either side of a table   and shared a pizza
and washed it down with a half-carafe of cheap red wine
and tried to talk their way back into their bodies
and as they left   the leaf-buds were a green promise

and when she stopped to put on more lipstick
she'd left it all printed around the rim of her glass
he laughed and said   There goes my chance to kiss you
Why   she replied   would you ever let that stop you
And they took each other's lips frankly   took their faces
between each other's hands   and the tears were shaken out
like raindrops beaded on a branch   and they were barely
able to have enough of touching   and they kissed each other dry
and over breakfast they smiled   so hard that it hurt

They went to make the bed   and found the sheets bloody
and so they fished through all their pockets for quarters   and walked
down to the corner laundromat   where they sat together
holding hands as they waited and watched the dryer tumble
Together they folded linen   billowed it out between them
to shake away the wrinkles   brought the corners together
in halves   in quarters   their bodies coming at each fold closer
and smiling at each other over the hot cotton

The clock-hand spun in circles   and soon morning was over
· and all they had left was the long drive to the airport
the slow walk through the terminal   trying to talk each other
out of sorrow   their voices bright with desperation
until they stood at the edge of what any words could comfort

Don't try to follow me this time she said   whatever
else happens   we made each other happy for a day
Yes he agreed   and they turned to walk away from each other
and though he struggled bravely to keep his face together
he cracked   he ran tear-broken back through the concourse
and caught her up in his arms   until she eased gently
out of his clasp   and kissed him one last time   and left him

But too late   the moment he turned   a demon of memory
sat hard on his shoulder and caught hold of his ear
murmuring over and over the words of their final parting
What   what would've given the story a happier ending

Out in the meadow that day   dark purple butterflies
sipped the sweet nectar from yellow cups of blossom
and blundered into the webs where the big spiders waited
to tuck them into the soft silk of their winding sheets
all their legs a wiggle of happy anticipation
What are you doing here she asked him   not unkindly
You look awful   your eyes are spilling over with memory

The world hurts to look at he said   all glitter and sharp edges
I'm sorry she said   but didn't I warn you to take your time
together   and let it go at that   it would've been kinder
Instead you sent your love back to my mansion   loaded
with twice the grief she left with   her own and yours also
And with that   he felt like he'd fallen into a dark lake
and the cold had got his bones   and he was slipping under
Let me join her then he said   I'm sick of living

No she told him   twice you've come here uninvited
and before I let you lay yourself in my bed forever
go back to the sunlit world   and tell your story
All I can offer you   if you aren't afraid to accept it
is a kind of consolation   and then she gave him a look
that was almost shy   First would you do me a small favor
Make me another song like the last one you sang me
only this time sing to me of self-effacing
surrender of love   that we give knowing we have to lose it

And so he sang of the love that is not so fearful of ending
that fear ends it   love that admits the flavor of pain
the pulling apart of ivy-tendrils ripped from a tree
love that lays itself in the grave of another body
sweetened by loss   as we lose ourselves in our lover's arms
given completely over to pleasure   the dark flower
that opens   petal by petal   unfolding us to the utmost
pitch of surrender   lost in the joy of self-forgetting

Then he praised the maiden who makes us a gift of grieving
to spill the bowl of our tears when it grows too heavy
the grace to release our beloved kindly into her care
and not to fear the soft tap of her footsteps approaching
her fingers touching our eyelids   when she comes to invite us
into her bed   and with cool unhurried hands unravels
the milky threads of our thoughts and memories   may we part with them
gladly   and go more easily into the dark flower

And the girl smiled   as if they'd shared a secret
and she broke the mullein-stalk in half and then in quarters
pressed the pieces into his palm and closed his fingers
Throw these to the wind she commanded   and he did
and they were lost in the long grass that cuts the ankles
Then she reached on her tiptoes   he was a head taller
and breathed into his mouth   the scent of mint and violets

And he woke up alone in the other world   and he was
walking down a familiar street   and it had been raining
all night   and the boughs of the trees were black and heavy
and the first cars of the morning passed   with their tires hissing
over the blacktop   and under his feet he felt the pavement
slither   a carpet of petals battered down by the raindrops
and each puddle swirled with a slick of green-gold pollen
and though he couldn't remember how or when it happened
his heart had been spilled   and at its quick was planted a wet
seed that he'd never known before   and it was spring

ADRIAN BLEVINS
The Brass Girl Brouhaha (2003)

Adrian Blevins' *The Brass Girl Brouhaha* won the 2004 Kate Tufts Discovery Award. Blevins is also the recipient of a Rona Jaffe Writers' Foundation Award, a Bright Hill Press Chapbook Award for *The Man Who Went out for Cigarettes,* and the Lamar York Prize for Nonfiction. A new book, *Live from the Homesick Jamboree,* is forthcoming from Wesleyan University Press. Blevins teaches at Colby College in Waterville, Maine.

In her own words: "Last year I would've said herein some fool thing about hybrid forms and sentence sounds and the not-passé I of the poor Seeing Eye. But that was then and this is now, eleven months after my son fell two stories off a roof on account of a sorry-assed ladder and the boy's probably barefoot and maybe some dew. And so forever now there is the ambulance and the rushing to the ICU and the fanatical horror of the pounding terror-now.

That is, though my son lives and has returned to school and is beautiful and funny and wise, what I know is me waiting in the hospital, wanting some help, some hope, some truth.

About the unacceptability of death!

About love's fierce counterattack!

About the overwhelmingness of having to live inside a body with a head on top.

About losing and losing and losing again, for during this time my father died—just stepped off the universe without so much as a wave goodbye.

And all I'm saying is: poetry, for me, was the help and the hope and the truth.

I'm incredibly grateful to Chase for making *The Brass Girl Brouhaha* audible to the world. But I don't know what to say about it. I wrote it out of fear. There is always too much to lose. It does get lost. We grieve."

LIFE HISTORY

I got this nose-shaped bruise on my left arm from falling into a
        rack of dolls at Wal-Mart.
This scar on my ring finger came from when I put my hand into
        a beehive when I was two,
a calamity about which I wept into Daddy's lissome clavicle for
        three and a half months.

As for the stretchmarks, don't ask about the stretchmarks.
        There are men who like them,
but men are liars making lairs, body-shaped soul-boats of
        stretchmark-making liquids
and big ideas about the beauty of women. I've been around. I
        know what makes a woman

beautiful. This scar under my eye is from when I played mouse
        with my cat Sebastian.
I am not sure how cats could leave a mark, but with me they do.
It's as though they wish to marry me or say *hello, hello*
        perpetually.

In photographs of me as a baby, I'm white space all over.
Now in this early fall of my thirty-eighth year there are freckles,
        moles,
and other assorted blotches. They say it's sun damage, maybe
        one day will be cancer.

Let us wait and see. When you get born, you're as blue as a
        bad painting of Saturn
in the middle of the night. When you're that blue, they might
        think you didn't make it.
They might think you opted out at the last minute, climbing a
        cable of light

to some spirit world fiesta. But really you're just getting the
        slow hang of gasping.
You're signing up for the Orientation, taking notes via the
        sluggish apparatus of your lungs
while they cut off the cord and take ten names for test drives.

Then you start to breathe. Then you turn pink. The more you
        wail, the pinker you get.
It's not the pink of salmon, and it's not the pink of tongue.
It's not the pink of the sunset or the pink of Matisse's "Portrait
        of Madame Matisse"

for I-don't-know-how-much money. This pink is the pink of the
        long inhale.
I know because I saw a dead woman who was chiefly dissected,
and she was the color of sand. I looked at her and felt nothing.

I wondered if she was Eskimo. I cut my toe here walking up the
    stairs.
I knocked my head against the medicine chest and thereby got
    indented.
My heart sometimes jumps and skips a beat. I don't know how I
    harmed it,

but I'm sure it was some blunder or another—one of the times
I took a pill, drank tequila, or gave birth against my will. Maybe it
    was when I told Daddy
my crying days were over and took up gulping stones.

But let's assume for the purposes of being accurate
that it was that long ago morning I first attempted speech,
burrowing out of myself like a sulky spider, climbing the cliff of
    unremitting self-infliction,

saying you—and you, and you, and you, and you—will one day
    pay for this.

APRIL SONG FOR AUGUST

Since it's spring again, the sun is at it again:
stripping all over the place all over the park.
It has untapped the keg and unfurled the licorice
and the minstrels. It's unfurled the blush,
people. It's blown the safe and looted the loot.
As for the old troubles, they're just laundry—
neither comic nor pathetic, neither news nor not.
That he says and she says. That the dogs mire
and the wells bite. That the handsome adolescents,
whom we've assembled, as well, and love,
as well, curse and smolder, just like other folks.
That we ourselves, for some odd reason,
clot and age so methodically. As for my daughter,
she's water, it's my job to keep her from spilling
over or out while she waddles along beside me
like a wild duck or a daisy or a dance,
since she really is a whole silliness of girl-babble
and blithe and founding and fleece. O child,
O delirious impossibility—bridge, dream, howl,
hitch—please come hear this meager salute.

NOVEMBER NEUROSIS

I am scared of varying my routine by even five minutes
because I'm scared of anything unsteady

because I'm scared of my children dying.

Car wrecks mostly, but burnings and drownings
and meningitis and leukemia and gunshots and bombings, as well.

That's how reckless the world is: it doesn't care to keep my
        children whole.

I was a giant moth in my white nursing gown
fluttering over my babies in their cribs.

I was a ghost, milky white—I'd lean down

and kiss their fleecy heads until they woke affronted.
Still I couldn't abide the dark room.

Still I *could not abide* that a man could ladder up and enter
        the unlockable room.

I'd put my babies in bed beside me then
and place my hand upon them to be sure they had heartbeats and
        pulses.

After some time my arm would throb and ache, but I would never
        move it.

The assorted husbands had to roll over or sleep on the floor
or Mastercard a King-sized bed! The assorted husbands

were immaterial unless they knew CPR.

Don't talk to me about sex, I'd say.
I'm checking her heart, I'm keeping him alive, I'm busy,
          don't talk.

I knew a girl whose brother killed her.

First he stabbed her, then he poured gasoline over her,
then he set her on fire.

In class not six months earlier

my students and I had admired the erotic energy of the girl's
          poem.
In class (not six months earlier)

the girl had put her eyes down and said, *but it's for my brother.*

He's in prison somewhere watching TV,
washing clothes, eating meat loaf.

I've thought of visiting. I've thought of saying: *Look, my
          babies are good—*

they'll do the world good, they're creative,
they pet stray dogs, they sing.

But so did his sister. She's buried, is all I'm saying.

She's lying solitary in a casket
like a black cricket under an empty counter.

She was *a child*, is all I'm saying.

The firemen found her and put her in a body bag.
I am forever worried and she is dead;

we are each of us born so holy and everlastingly molested.

STILL LIFE WITH PEEVED MADONNA

It's clear I'm standing on the Isle of Motherdom
given these three children hanging off my arms and feet

weighing the weight of the planet, at least.
The children look like dime-store bric-a-brac

since all that swings will squarely star-sparkle,
but more like missiles in size and expulsion intent.

They're asking how cold is the water, to which I say I don't know.
They're asking could they have some macaroni & cheese

to which I say I'm occupied hating this line, hush, now hush.
They're asking how far is it inland & do the natives dance there

& can they go & get some confetti & snort or inject it
to which I say years ago I could answer your questions

but look at those clouds, I think that's a cyclone
to which they say, fuck you, Mom, you're always so paranoid

to which I say, fuck you, too, you remind me of lizards,
were you birthed in an outhouse by an ogre or a loon?

LAURE-ANNE BOSSELAAR
A New Hunger (2007)

Laure-Anne Bosselaar is the author of *The Hour Between Dog and Wolf* and *Small Gods of Grief,* winner of the Isabella Gardner Prize for Poetry. Ausable Press published her third book, *A New Hunger,* which was selected as an ALA Notable Book in 2008. She is also the recipient of a Pushcart Prize. Bosselaar is the editor of *Outsiders: Poems about Rebels, Exiles and Renegades, Urban Nature: Poems about Wildlife in the City,* and *Never Before: Poems about First Experiences.* She and her husband, poet Kurt Brown, completed a book of translations from Flemish poet Herman de Coninck: *The Plural of Happiness.* She teaches at Sarah Lawrence College, and at the Low Residency MFA in Creative Writing Program of Pine Manor College.

In her own words: "I'm obsessed by the powers of imagery: how random images (a face, swirl in the river, a seed) so often plant deep emotional hooks in me, and bring forth a nexus of other connections, at first mysterious, but almost always their links reveal themselves in the writing process.

Having grown up in an environment where nurturing and any kind of closeness or intimacy were severely discouraged , I have an almost maniacal fascination about discovering how people live—well . . . to be totally honest, how people *survive*. In 'Man at the Museum of Modern Art' I describe how I 'stalk' people: and how this 'spying' teaches me how I am linked and part of the human community. And these welcome connections are always taught to me by an image— sometimes even a tiny detail in an image. This 'imagistic inner-life' is my way to connect, to feel included in humankind.

This process of discovery is probably most obvious in the double crown of sonnets 'The River's Mouth, the Boat, the Undertow'— where the constant repetition of images plays an essential role in— here comes that word again!—connecting the fourteen poems that are part of this sequence.

All the poems in this book are also connected by a conscious deci- sion to keep the language simple, but resonant. English is the third language in which I write, and it is still new enough for me to revel in playing with its music and cadences. And it is with this 'noise' that I give emphasis to the tone in each poem—paying immense (and loving!) attention to the impact of alliteration, assonance and syntax. And finally, what was quite a 'dare' for me, I decided that I would allow myself to break some rules, and introduce, often in the same poem a link (notice I didn't use 'connection'!) of narrative, lyric and meditative elements."

FRIENDS,

this is the viscous heart I hide from you:
gnashing, polluted, hooked to my ribs
like a burr, stuck there and stinging,
and it's only four fourteen in the morning.

Those sudden shudders my waking alarm,
then the daily discipline of shutting away that heart,
shambling through the house, touching things,
stroking their shapes as if it could help me

not be the Bad Sower's daughter each morning:
the pit from a seed he sowed and left to parch,
and no crows would feed on it. So I lived. I don't
want to explain this further, I'm done with it.

But this for you: on the days I touch your books,
read your letters, recall a gaze, the delicate
dangle of an earring, or the throwing
back of a head in laughter,

it's you seeding the first beat into the heart
I open. And as the sun heaves daylight
into the parched tree by my window,
and rats burrow away; when pigeons come

down to feed on dust and pizza crusts, I thrum
the lit syllables of your names on my sill with all
ten fingers, typing them firmly into the brick,
and counting their beats, counting their beats.

ELEGY

The past lies in the swath I left
crossing a summer meadow in Belgium.

I wanted to see my old house one
last time, and crossed the field at dawn.

Some grasses lifted their heads
after my passage—wild chamomile and chervil—

but the touch-me-not lay crushed.
I found nothing there I wanted to bring back

and no one was left to see me turn away.

NIGHT

Lights go off, one by one, in buildings
across the street. There's something

solemn about this—the lone
drone of cars and cabs

an urban lullaby to shut windows.

Pull the sheet over this day, subway driver,
torah reader, birthday girl, pimp.

Pull the sheet, soldier's mother, corpse
dresser, drunk man's bride.

Sleep my daughter. Sleep my son,

and sleep Jeremiah Smith: the newborn
he delivered in a charity ward today. Sleep.

Wrap a wing around the orphan,
the hungry woman, the caged man.

Shut your eyes, face your walls, the scythe's

blade is tilting toward the earth—so
sleep for the one who knows horror,

or the one who dares speak in any god's name.

Don't listen to the clockmaker: he's setting
the alarm. Sleep until it rings—sleep

toward the waking and the windowless night.

STILLBIRTH

On a platform, I heard someone call out your name:
No, Laetitia, no.
It wasn't my train—the doors were closing,
But I rushed in, searching for your face.

But no Laetitia. No.
No one in that car could have been you,
but I rushed in, searching for your face:
no longer an infant. A woman now, blond, thirty two.

No one in that car could have been you.
Laetitia-Marie was the name I had chosen.
No longer an infant. A woman now, blond, thirty two:
I sometimes go months without remembering you.

Laetitia -Marie was the name I had chosen:
I was told not to look. Not to get attached—
I sometimes go months without remembering you.
Some griefs bless us that way, not asking much space.

I was told not to look. Not to get attached.
It wasn't my train—the doors were closing.
Some griefs bless us that way, not asking much space.
On a platform, I heard someone calling your name.

From THE RIVER'S MOUTH,
THE BOAT, THE UNDERTOW

She listens to music, eyes closed, hands joined, headset
lost in thick black curls. A button on her jean jacket reads
Still Against The War. Next to her on the bus,

a small boy frowns, mouthing something to his plastic
police car. Now and then he looks up at an older woman
who has been staring at them for a while. That's
all I'll ever know about them.

All I'll ever know is that we traveled a few blocks together
and nothing happened. What thoughts they had, what
the child mouthed, what music the woman listened to—

insignificant. Right? It was only *me* thinking the boy wanted
to shoot the class bully from that cop car, right? Or imagining
the older woman was a racist, and the other a dreamer.
What would you have seen? What would you have thought?

    *

What would you have seen? What would you have thought
watching those two men crossing the Brooklyn Bridge, *shrill
shirts ballooning,* trying to understand each other, hands

swooping up the air like gulls. That the poets *gave each other
wisdom or love or even a good time* isn't the point—it's that
no one crossing them on the bridge that day recognized them,
or stopped in awe to watch Crane and Lorca walk by.

No one noticed Crane and Lorca walk by, they weren't stars,
presidents, pitchers or popes after all—only two men standing
with empty hands in the murmur of the rivers' mouth.

The two greatest poetic geniuses alive meet, and what
happens? What did they see, what did they talk about,
feel, or think then, as around them the air, clouds and
waters went on shuffling chance and light?

                    *

Waters went on shuffling chance and light as the boy
jumped into the river. He had come home from school
that day with a drawing for his dad and found him

overdosed on the couch. The Czech have a word for what
drowned the boy. For what it is that guts a woman's belly
long after an abortion; a word for what hurts, exactly,
when a sheet is pulled over a child, mother, soldier.

In sheets pulled over a child or soldier, there is *litost.*
At the auction of his tractor, *litost* plows a farmer's heart.
In bombs strapped to a terrorist's chest or in the guns

pointed at him—*litost.* Kundera tells us it's untranslatable,
that we have no word for this in English. But here's the point—
what if we did? Would a word make pain more tolerable?
As if language could help.

[Note: *In the seventh sonnet of "The River's Mouth, the Boat, the Undertow" I gratefully*
stole phrases from Hart Crane, Federico Garcia Lorca, and Philip Levine.]

GARAGE SALE

I sold her bed for a song.
A song of yearning like an orphan's.
Or the one knives carve into bread.

But the un-broken bread
song too. For the song that a river
sings to the ferryman's oars—with

that dread in it.
For a threadbare tune: garroted,
chest-choked, cheap. A sparrow's,

beggar's, a foghorn's call.
For the kind of song only morning
can slap on love-stained sheets—

that's what I sold my mother's
bed for. The one she died in. Sold it
for a song.

ROBERT BOYERS
A Book of Common Praise (Essays, 2002)

Robert Boyers is Editor of the quarterly *Salmagundi*, Director of The New York State Summer Writers Institute and Professor of English at Skidmore College. Among his nine books the most recent are *The Dictator's Dictation: Essays on the Politics of Novels and Novelists* and *Excitable Women, Damaged Men*, a volume of short stories.

In his own words: "For more than forty years I have been delivering substantial literary introductions at public readings and lectures, for writers as various as Robert Lowell and Joseph Brodsky, Susan Sontag and Nadine Gordimer, Saul Bellow and Seamus Heaney. At one point, when Chase Twichell recommended that I put together a book of these introductions, I discovered that I had saved the hand-written originals of nearly a thousand such pieces, each between 600 and 850 words. The book I then assembled contains a hundred of the best of the introductions, frequently including multiple takes on favorite writers like Robert Pinsky and Frank Bidart in poetry, or Michael Ondaatje, Russell Banks and J.M. Coetzee in fiction. The writers I've introduced have often told me how much they enjoy being brought on with a carefully measured though inevitably enthusiastic fanfare. And when the book itself came out, other writers and critics wrote that they thought I had made 'shrewd and sensible' judgments while also managing occasionally to be 'funny' and even 'challenging to [their] own assumptions.' Clearly the pieces in the collection are not expansive or in any way academic essays but miniatures attempting to provide what Chase Twichell calls 'sharp insight into the writer's work, placing it on the literary map' and, striving somehow to 'encapsulate an entire career, charting a writer's structural, musical, philosophical, and political evolution by tracking the subtle ghost of the human imagination.' Do the pieces succeed? I say, in my introduction to a book of introductions, that I want there to breathe in each of them 'the love of good writing and of honest writerly ambition,' and that is as much as I will allow myself to claim."

on C.K. WILLIAMS (1999)

C. K. Williams doesn't write pretty poems. With rare exception he abjures the ornamental, the fastidious, the polished phrase, the neat emblematic finish of the master craftsman conscious of his mastery and eager to impress. His is a poetry of struggle and voice, prickly and introspective, worldly and engaged. To read the poems is to feel enlarged, challenged, more than occasionally disturbed, surprised by sudden eruptions of meaning, bewildered by the capacious sympathies and hungers of an imagination that can move so readily from certitude to suspicion, from tenderness to pain, from anecdote to soaring reflection. It is no wonder that other poets marvel at the rage for truthfulness, or truth-telling, or candor, in a body of work that wears not only its emotions but its doubts and reluctances and ideas and convictions very much on its long, battered sleeves.

The manic flutter of the poetry is often its most obvious and strangely beguiling attribute—strange because it is not often that insistent struggle can seem so humanly appealing, so fully an expression of a becoming will to get at the truth of things, to unmask the secrets of the heart, to bring pressure to bear on every least and large particular so as to reveal what should be known. The insistence comes in many forms. There is the repetition of key words and phrases, a sudden recourse to an illuminating, obsessively worked, lavishly exfoliating metaphor, or a compulsive re-tracing of the terrain, with every sense along the way that, no matter how often you correct and start again and press forward, you are likely to want to have another go at the conundrums and anxieties that stir you to wonder and to feel. Even when the poet is confident, coming at last, or at first, to a conclusion—"not suspicion, / mind, conclusion, / not a doubt about it, not a hesitation," as he tells us in a brilliant poem called "Signs," the speaker in a Williams poem is ever on the edge of doubt, alert to the fact that a part of what he is after will be "hard to track," the more obvious things what you "can just make out," the truths revealed apt to be "forgotten, absolutely," too much for our drifting, doubting minds to hold onto. And so the manic urgency in the poems is a manifest of the poet's perpetual susceptibility to puzzlement, his inability or unwillingness to leave anything alone, his attachment to the interrogative, so that *maybe* and *why* and *but* and *wouldn't it* and *mightn't this* and even *yes. no. yes* constitute an inescapable feature of his rhetoric and his outlook.

To be sure, there are occasional poems in which Williams is not so entirely a voluptuary of anxiety, not so insistently a diver into the wreck as a patient explorer of latency. Some of the poems in his latest book, *Repair*, even look slight, almost neat, shapely on the page, with occasional short lines, though it wouldn't take a lot to adjust the lineage and create at once the impression of amplitude and flux and reversal that seems so central to this poet's work, with its characteristic long lines and dialectical tensions, its proliferating adjectives and retards, its intensifiers and qualifiers. There is room in Williams' work for the odd occasional poem, for the small thing that seems, just for a moment, an exception, but in truth there is in the body of the work, surely as it has evolved over the last twelve or fifteen years, an unmistakable accent that has made the poems seem to us so vital, a part of the way many of us think about ourselves. The accent can accommodate love and grief and pity and nostalgia, but it is not principally derived from the will to express those lively or lugubrious emotions. It is the accent, rather, of thought itself, of thought working through the full range of emotions that call it into being. It is the accent of the mind—call it soul, if you will—arguing with itself, discovering how and why we feel as we do, pressing forward, tumbling back, accumulating memories and conjectures and, when necessary, letting them go, then gathering force again, readying, up for the next foray into the stuff of the common experience, shifting its feet to locate reliable terra firma, learning what to call this thing or that, often disappointed or agitated, almost never still or secure, breathing hard, breathing soft, but coiled always to receive some new burst of information, some refreshment of feeling, some access of bewilderment or insight.

Of course we say of such a poet—we can't deny that we are tempted—that he is a philosopher-poet, a psychologist, that his medium is thought, that his gift is for translating experience into emotion and idea. But this is not a man bent on bringing home hard-won nuggets of analysis or wisdom. His gift is not for system or theory but for journeying out and journeying in, with no prospect of completion. The poems of C.K. Williams are at once relentless and generous, prepared to take us through the next labyrinth, and the next, attuned to portents, attentive to things spiritual and debased, prepared to uncover the worst we can imagine about ourselves, but ever alert to the possibility of atonement, absolution, forgiveness, connection. Best to say of this poet that he is acquainted with the night and strong enough to bring to us, now and again, the morning light. This is a poet who delivers the buried life and the ordinary satisfactions into vivid consciousness.

on ROBERT PINSKY (2001)

In an essay in *The Sacred Wood* T.S. Eliot describes, as best he can, the honesty he takes to be an essential feature of genuine poetry. "It is," he writes, "a peculiar honesty, which in a world too frightened to be honest, is peculiarly terrifying. It is an honesty against which the world conspires because it is unpleasant." I quote these sentiments because I happened upon them the other day, not for the first time, and I couldn't help thinking that Robert Pinsky would probably resist them, very much as I do. This is no small thing. Eliot was, I believe, an honest man, or at least an honest poet, one who used poetry to imagine and discover and tell what he took to be the truth. And Robert Pinsky, likewise, seems to me, in that sense precisely, a completely honest poet, never frivolous, never less than a truth-seeker and, with all the ironic self-awareness the task often entails, a truth-teller.

But what of Eliot's idea that the genuine poet works "in a world too frightened to be honest" and which therefore finds the poet's work "terrifying"? Pinsky has been writing poems for several decades now, and often he has turned his attention to painful subjects. But he has not written, so far as we can tell, with a sense that his peculiar honesty would seem to the world terrifying. There is, in Robert's work, no sense of an unbridgeable gap between self and other, no pride of alienated majesty to elevate the poet's self-esteem and confirm for him the impossible inadequacy of the little terrified earthlings, that is to say, his readers. His honesty is not, in its essence, an affair of pride at all. It is, rather, a reflection of the poet's conviction that the value we have for ourselves depends upon our willingness, where possible, to call things by their rightful names, to acknowledge and live with unsatisfiable desires, to make and unmake and remake, and never ever to suppose that there lies, just around the next corner, some final consolation or irrevocable single truth.

Of course it is hard to read Eliot's lines about honesty in poetry and relate them to the varieties of ordinary pleasure Robert's poems rehearse for us. To suppose, with Eliot, that the world "conspires"—that is

Eliot's word—conspires against the poet and the honesty he would practice is to be, as a poet, suspicious, potentially bitter. The poet, or persona, who speaks in Robert's work is neither bitter nor, by disposition, suspicious. His is not what is sometimes called an unhappy consciousness, poised always to recoil from the world, which the unhappy consciousness regards as fatally unlovely, disappointing. The honesty of Robert's poems is an expression of his openness to possibility and to hope, of his willingness to believe that things may sometimes turn out to be better than they seem, or that from bitterest despair there may emerge something valuable, if only an enhanced understanding of what it is to be human. Like William Carlos Williams, a poet for whom Robert has an especial fondness, he ranges freely over a wide range of emotions, occasionally taking his own pulse, but mostly attentive to the lives of others and the tumultuous life of the culture in all of its dimensions. There is never in Robert's work anything condescending or impatient, and though he might not quite agree with Williams that, as Randall Jarrell wrote, "The differences between men are less important than their similarities," he is never less than clear-eyed and delicately discerning, as willing to admire where admiration is required as to observe and register what is ugly or indecent.

We would not, surely, say that in Robert there is an "invincible joyousness," but there are in all of Robert's books surprising accessions of "fresh gaiety," "a wonderful largeness" of spirit, a willingness to acknowledge and invite tenderness, and also, no doubt about it, a tough unsentimental candor. Detachment is but one important strategy in Robert's work, wit and humor leavening agents in a poetry that is never ponderous, ever fleet in its motions, but richly musical, resonant, the carefully tuned instrument of a "perfection"—I almost close here with words from a Pinsky poem—a "perfection imagined just before unperfecting / itself as if by impulse."

In that impulse—to unperfect the imagined perfection, to roughen the surface of a mellifluous line, to tell a joke and fit it exactly to the purposes of elegy, to mix high and low, jazz idiom and elevated diction, homely sentiment and spiritual yearning—in that unperfecting is Robert Pinsky's perfect honesty.

on SEAMUS HEANEY (1992)

"Is it any wonder," Seamus Heaney asks in a poem called "Terminus,"
"when I thought / I would have second thoughts?" No wonder, to
be sure, for us, faithful readers of poems marked, from the first, by
many varieties of second thoughts, misgivings, self-doubts, recoils
and conditionals. A lover of exuberance and release, an admirer of
the "wandering voice" and a poetry of "pure play," Seamus is, at the
same time, a stern moralist—stern at least in self-interrogation and
in scrupulous self-correction. This is a poet adept, as he has often
intimated, at "suffering the limit of each claim." And what is that
limit, we may ask, if not that margin where doubt encroaches upon
assertion, where the road robustly taken suddenly looks like a road
shadowed by "dreaded omen" or "evil eye."

Seamus's poetry is very much in touch with myth and legend, but it is not a poetry infatuated with magic or tempted by su-
perstition. It is ever in search of plausible epiphanies and clarifica-
tions, but wary of grand or blinding illuminations. The world, in
Seamus's poetry, can be a great good place, but it is also a place of
abrasions and resignations, where, to be fully alive, is to feel one-
self tested, one's ordinary tendency to moderation and "decency" at
least intermittently subjected to derision. The poet himself, so he
suggests, may not be—or not always—the one "whose boat will lift
when the cloudburst happens," but he will more than occasionally
stand his modest ground, resist the bland imperatives to equivocate,
swerve, apologize.

Even in his great 1975 volume, *North*, we were let in on a
dark, unresolveable tension in Seamus's outlook, a tension reflected in the marrow of his diction and the rhythm of his speech. In
North the tension was felt in the disparity between the tendency
to bluntness and astringency, on the one hand, and the pervasive,
unimpeachable fellow-feeling everywhere apparent even in poems
notable for what the poet calls their "iron composition" and their
resistance to nostalgia.

Of course there are many varieties of tension in Seamus's work, and the tenor of the most memorable poems in *North* is quite different from the tenor of the major poems in *Station Island* or *The Haw Lantern*. In section four of the long sequence called "Clearances," the tenor is retrospective, anecdotal, albeit with a formal stringency imposed by the sonnet form, but the tension is harder to name. Clearly it has something to do with a diction that is at once precise and yet surprising in the liberties it affords itself. Clearly, too, the tenson is reflected in the poet's dual commitment to truth-telling, on the one hand, and to the tender, humane retrospection that naturally informs a sequence written in memory of the poet's mother.

We register the tension most sharply in the poet's handling of the word "betrayal," where the word designates the poet's willingness to go along with his mother's fear of affectation and her aversion to sophistication or elegance, in short to the artfulness and refinements of the poet himself. And so the poet would, as he says, "naw and aye / And decently relapse into the wrong/ Grammar which kept us allied and at bay." Charming, and not a little disturbing, that clinching "allied and at bay," but not quite so disturbing and unforgiving as the earlier words, "So I governed my tongue / In front of her, a genuinely well- /adjusted adequate betrayal /of what I knew better." Nothing so sharply captures, I think, the poet's dual commitments, his inveterate, compulsive gift for second thoughts, his deep misgivings, even about his own command of language and idiom, as that line naming the "genuinely well- / adjusted adequate betrayal."

Was ever the genuine so well and authentically matched with the idea of betrayal as it is in Seamus's poem? Was ever the word 'adequate' so entirely a concession to frailty, the "well-adjusted" so bluntly an admission of an ordinary gift for trimming and accommodation? We feel, in such a poem, the war within the poet, his struggle to be decent and better than decent, to own up while doing his best not to unduly wound or confound, his delicate efforts at balance, charity and proportion tested by a contrary instinct to expose, to estrange himself and his reader from the familiar and the comfortable, to resist sleepwalk and every variant of the folded lie.

Seamus Heaney has helped us to understand, more than any poet we know, the meaning of the struggle to identify "right action" and to offer an "uncompromised report" of one's own motives and experience. No poet has given us poems at once so tenderly responsive to the ordinary life we lead and, at the same time, so alert to the several "grammar(s) of imperatives" that make of the good life a constant test. Can I be equal, will I be equal, have I been equal— so Seamus's poems would seem in their many ways to ask—equal to what is demanded of me if I am to think well of myself? With no trace of merely "adequate" self-justification, with no posturing displays of moral rectitude, Seamus's poems represent the most powerful interrogation of our common life that we have had in the last quarter of the twentieth century.

JULIANNE BUCHSBAUM
Slowly, Slowly, Horses (2001)

Julianne Buchsbaum earned an MFA from the Iowa Writers' Workshop in 1999, where she was the recipient of a Paul Engle Fellowship from the James Michener Foundation. Her poems have appeared or are forthcoming in various journals, including *Conduit, Verse, The Journal, Southwest Review, Delmar* and *Harvard Review* and are anthologized in *Legitimate Dangers: American Poets of the New Century* and *A Best of Fence: The First Nine Years.* Her work won the 1999 Randall Jarrell Poetry Prize and has been nominated several times for a Pushcart Prize. Ms. Buchsbaum lives and works in Lawrence, Kansas.

In her own words: "I was once asked who the ideal reader of my poems would be. My answer is that my ideal reader does not want an easy ride. My ideal reader wants the poem to put him or her in danger; he or she wants to risk something 'elemental' when reading. My ideal reader allows him or herself to be seized by the poem as by some inexplicable force or phenomenon that cannot be reduced or explained away by a detached and cynical intellect. My ideal reader is interested in self-overcoming and is open to the ways in which languages, etymologies, the structures and sounds of words, phrases, images, tropes, and figurations can take part in this overcoming."

ANECDOTE OF A MANICHAEAN

No character who's kind
in this tale of what the mind
can do to the body.

Life, the old imposter,
sank under the cragged plaster
of its ponderous effigy.

Is it true that ennui
can really be just a need
for water? Mentally

there's a slow inversion:
the self's alarming version
of its enemy.

It went from simple white
to cataclysmic night:
that strange, erratic sky.

The mind can't apprehend
that what should never end
is always passing by.

The body knows the truth
despite its terrified, mute
rehearsal of the lie.

QUEEN OF ULTIMA THULE

Here in the ultima Thule of my mind,
I no longer think of you. I left you in my sleep,
in the throne I established for you there.
When dawn eased its pallor between the blinds,

my mouth was dry. Far below this mountain
with its ice-cream cool, its undulant planes
and royal blues, I see the shadows teeming.
Dust turns to mud in the yellow rain below.

Once I held a poppy, red as a beggar's eye.
That flower was the oriflamme of my striving.
I crouched beneath the pelting rain while
some new suffering whirled beneath my skin.

And this is the kingdom bestowed on me
by your mouth and its crimes and perils.
Here there are no shadows. At the apex
I tear at with my pick-ax, all is ice and steel.

GAMBLERS

You doze in a castle of eggshells, Tartar,
while rain soaks the cornfields outside.
This is not about me; I have nothing to do with it.

Who are you, ruminating in the corner like that?
The bar is dark; it's time to go home.
Stop ransacking the past for what ruined you.

See, outside, how the sweet cicely holds
its tiny white umbrellas in the storm?
You thought you were safe here?

Alumroot blanches the roadside from here
to wherever you're going.
Nodules that no one but you knows are alive,

lives that are their own reason for being,
with the whiteness of what is thrown open
to the dead silence of the universe.

While someone faces the hazards of loving you,
the clouds overhead foam like boiling milk
and you turn solemn and cold and formal.

Somewhere the sea drags itself over the faces
of the drowned. Somewhere gamblers
are cutting their losses as another day slips by.

A HOUSE OF CARDS

I suppose we were dis-
illusioned and chilled,
but what a lovely time

was had by all: a clear
night, early winter,
a party ensuing in the

building next door,
the young valets dashing
down the alley yelling;

an expectation of new things,
the banishment of death
and unmentionables.

We called for an encore
of noble reasoning
in the dining hall, with our

destiny unknown for the night,
and the high loves of
the hostess revealed

to all and sundry—who
danced with the fervor,
that night, of orphans.

AIRS OF MIDDLE NIGHT

The sky pokes a black finger
through a wormhole in a leaf

where a nightingale's eye had glinted.
We no longer speak of the sky,

though carnations tilt in a vase:
a clump of shunted hydra-heads,

they reek of astrology.
The nightingale no longer sings

where snakes jerk through convolutions
of dead petals, though a tint

of its plumage flares
across the sky and lingers

like the perfume of a woman
who has rushed from the room.

CLOUDS SWELL OUT

The finale of fall hangs in yellow clusters.
You can't muster

the drive required for potent acts—to hide
like the cat who eyed

each skittering leaf and churring sparrow from
a dark sanctum,

frozen, invisible, dumb—such is your will.
The world is ill

with demands it can't meet; hence, the crickets'
deaths, the rosettes

of rot, the dusky clusters, and flourishing worms.
All this confirms

your wish to divorce yourself from the vista
and phenomena

of autumn which looms from raw branches a dark
afternoon. The stark

landscape deepening its shadowed dales cannot
stray a lot

from the invincible doctrine, though owls moan
misgivings. Alone,

you watch a jet's contrail zip open the sky
and the high

clouds swell out like huge, snowy hearts disgorged.

MISÈRE DES HÔTELS

Amok in the dialectic mess of the streets,
its mad choreography of hands and feet,

how can I look at the sky and not want it?
Its star-tortured skin so far out of whack

with signs of a storm before the storm comes.
Day after day I don my face like a uniform.

Amok in the oceanic gross-out of roaches,
broken meats—the palaces of Machu Picchu

despoiled of lavishness and the black ware
of lesser gods and a silver llama—I, an heir

to this legacy of track-lit chaff and char,
this potsherd world of power-lunch smut.

Love is a speck in these boroughs of glitz
defaced with each night's graffiti. How will I

know who speaks when you turn to me from
the ex nihilos of your mind? When the city

opens its drains, even the dead are displaced,
orphaned and spreading their tarnished coins.

SCARRED

Clouds flake off piece by piece above the rough
ice-collared snow, the slags of light in soil.

The splay of tree-crowns spurring and furling
up into the sky. Black boughs in glacial ache.

Husks of bark, of shivered wood moored on ice;
fringe of it receding from pools of blue,

the pools having taken the sheen of sky
down to their depths. Palest of white ridges

infolding, asphalt bastioned with furrows
along the field of it. Scarred with dead blades,

the world withdraws in white before me.
Frost's multi-angled effacements—nothing

made fast is what I have: the atrophy
of leaf and sap, the waste and feed of it.

HAYDEN CARRUTH
Letters to Jane (2004)

Hayden Carruth published more than thirty books, mostly poetry. He won numerous prizes for his work, including the National Book Award for Poetry, the Lenore Marshall Award, the Paterson Poetry Prize, the Whiting Award, the Ruth Lilly Prize, and a Lannan Literary Fellowship. He died in 2008 as *An Ausable Reader* was going to press.

In his own words: "To my mind, this era in the evolution of American civilization is actually an appalling devolution. Our culture is coming apart. What could be more antithetical to the fostering of art and literature? Artists now bear a greater burden than ever before. We must continually disprove the efficacy of violence and greed in human affairs. We must continuously dissuade our fellow citizens from supporting the program of violence and greed which has been foisted on us. And we must, in honor and honesty, continuously criticize and castigate persons in our society who have raised and sustained this program. Far more than the well-being of art and literature is at stake in our endeavors. We are the vindicators of good sense in our nation. Our voices will resonate throughout the world." —from an interview with John Amen in *Pedestal Magazine*

April 25, 1994

Dear Jane,
It's an entirely typical morning here. Gray, drizzly, warm, a song sparrow in the old grape vine, crows congregating noisily in the woods.
I've been up for about an hour and a half. I've made coffee and fed
the cats, Mudgins and Cooker, I've drunk two mugs of coffee and
smoked six or seven cigarettes, I've considered my sins, and now I'm
sitting in my tattered old wingback chair by the stove (cold at this
time of year) with my new portable computer on my knees. Much
more comfortable than sitting stark upright at the desk. Joe-Anne is
still sleeping. We were up late last night, as we are most nights.

We heard the rumor of your illness a couple of weeks ago, but from
a source I thought might not be reliable. We were thinking of ways
to confirm or disconfirm it without asking directly, which seemed
too clumsy, and finally Joe-Anne wrote Don a letter that he would
have to answer—he would have anyway, of course—and now we
know. We've both been devastated. We've wept and raged. Of all
the blows to our sense of propriety and natural rectitude that we've
sustained in the past few years, this is the worst by far. I don't know
what to say. I know you are in pain and extremely uncomfortable,
so I can't wish you anything on that account. I know you are coura-
geous and stubborn. I know you are remarkably intelligent and that
your intelligence is the kind which includes good sense. I know your
mind possesses immense resources of imaginative energy. About all
I can do (unless you tell me otherwise) is reassure you of our love,
Joe-Anne's and mine. It is compounded of natural affinity, gratitude,
and admiration. It is great and active.

I remember the first time you and I met, at least I think it was the first,
before I met you with Don. You were doing a reading in Syracuse.

We had lunch together at a restaurant called O'Toole's, where the dining area is a balcony surrounding a lower room in which the bar is located. It bothered my acrophobia, and we sat at a table as far from the railing as we could get. Immediately we knew we were kin, so to speak. We talked about psychogenic disabilities in a tough, laughing way, comparing experiences. It was a reinforcing thing for us, warm with the bonding that comes from mutuality of suffering and temperament—I think I had already reviewed a couple of your books—the sort of understanding that revives instantaneously whenever and however infrequently we meet, as it has.

Don't think about answering this. Use your good time for getting strong and writing poems. I will write again soon. Tomorrow I must go down to D.C. to do a reading, about which I'm a little apprehensive because I was in the hospital myself recently for an operation and don't feel altogether up to it, but I'm sure I'll be all right and I'll be back home the next day.

With love, HC

April 30, 1994

Dear Jane,

I arrived in Syracuse at about 5:00 yesterday but somehow was waylaid by friends who plied me with pineapple juice and hors d'oeuvres made from dogfood and bits of coal until I was utterly stinko. I am still in Syracuse. Joe-Anne will come and get me later on. I am sitting in a leather easy chair with my feet on a fine Bokara carpet, smoking cigarettes, drinking coffee and whiskey, my little computer, which is called "Hayden's Toy," plugged into the wall beside me—one's constant connection. Where would we be without our baseboard outlets? The house is empty except for me and one delightful child named Clio, who is upstairs in bed with a fever. No one seems to know what's the matter with her. General dissatisfaction, I expect.

I think of us, our little gang, as refugees, not so much from the world, which used to be our enemy but now just ignores us, as from the "literary community," which fears us. I saw this in Washington. Very nice young people who treated me well, but I could tell from their questions that what they really want is for me to get out of the way, me with my old-fashioned notions of honesty and compassion. "How can you possibly love a heron?" they say. "Such a ridiculous, filthy bird—and obsolete at that." And how can I answer? My poems convince them momentarily; their eyes shine, their faces blush. But then in an instant they recover themselves and reject all my nonsense.

Incidentally I have become a splendid performer. Who could have foreseen that? It surprises everyone who knows me, including myself. I didn't give my first reading until I was 58 years old.

May 9, 1994

Dear Jane,
Monday morning. Warm and bright. At this time of day the sun shines through the kitchen window and hits my chair. So I bask like a cat while I'm having my coffee and cigarettes. Joe-Anne is down in Jersey to see her family, especially her son Adam, and I'm alone for a couple of weeks, which always makes me haywire—depressed and desperate at the same time. I know you know what I mean. (Joe-Anne doesn't want me to go with her on these visits and I've never met any of her family except Adam—but that's another story.) So I frittered away the weekend: read a short manuscript, wrote a few letters, watched a hell of a lot of basketball, read what we used to call cheap-screw fiction. I haven't heard that term for a while. At first it meant under-the-counter porn, but later came to mean any escapist literature. As a consequence, on top of the desperation and depression I feel guilt. What else is new?

Well, it's the start of a new week and maybe I can get myself on track.

It's tulip time and I've seen some marvelous displays in people's yards, including a couple in my own. It's also insect time. The black flies up in the woods are fierce, the house has been invaded by new legions of ants and spiders. When I woke this morning a small, very delicate spider was on the wall about six inches from my head. I put on my glasses and looked at it. Long graceful legs like a ballet dancer's. Unafraid and poised. I blew at it gently and I swear it turned around and looked at me, though even with my glasses I couldn't see its eyes. A nice little greeting in the morning from the world to me. I'm reminded of when I was a soldier in Italy 50 years

Well, the lady of the house, Isabel, who is a Chilean refugee and whom I love dearly, has come home for lunch and Joe-Anne will be here before long. Members of the little gang. I could not survive without them.

Love again, HC

or more ago. We used to sleep in mosquito bars because of the malaria (which most of us got anyway), and often in the morning when I woke up there'd be a little Italian lizard on the netting about six inches above my face. Looking, at that distance, like a dinosaur. Another nice little greeting. If you moved very slowly you could sometimes tickle their bellies and they seemed to like it.

Well, the cats are demanding their breakfast. Their proper names are Cookie (because she is black and white like an Oreo, named by Adam when she was a kitten) and Smudge (because she is all white except for a little gray patch on her head that wouldn't wash off when I took her in as a filthy starved waif three years ago), but normally they are called Cooker and Mudgins. Cooker is a very old cat now and has metal replacements in her hind quarters from the time when she was hit by a car, so she walks with a wobble and complains from time to time; but she's still good-looking and very affectionate. Mudgins is handsome, in the prime of life, haughty, superior, yet she follows me around like a dog and always stays within sight distance. When I'm working she sleeps on my worktable. I'm thinking about getting a dog, which I've wanted ever since I came to Munnsville. I've held off because the highway that runs past our house is heavily traveled by cars and trucks going at high speed and I've seen too many animals killed on the wayside. But perhaps I can find a way to overcome that risk. It will take patience. But I have this summer mostly free to stay at home, and training a dog would be a good thing to do.

Jane, I know you're going through every kind of hell. I know there's nothing I can say about it that you don't know. I'm as sorry as I can be, devastated, and I'm thinking of you a lot. I hope my silly letters don't seem offensive to you.

With much love, HC

May 20, 1994

Dear Jane,

Joe-Anne returned last night, and with her came Stacey—that's
what I've decided to call her. It's not the name she has borne hereto-
fore, which I don't like, but close enough; she recognizes it. She re-
sembles a somewhat overgrown red fox. I'd say she must have some
Irish setter in her background, but she's a good deal smaller than a
setter and must have a lot of other things in her too. Her ears stand
up but not pointedly, her eyes are brown, so is her nose, she has a
fine brushy tail, etc. The main thing is that she is very friendly, took
to me and this house immediately, spent the night placidly, seems
unperturbed by her sudden transplantation.

The cats are another matter. Cooker has stayed in the kitchen and
doesn't mind Stacey as long as she doesn't come too near, and then
she, Cooker, hisses and lashes out. Mudgins has remained upstairs
the whole time so far, ready to dash under the bed if danger ap-
proaches. I don't like this; dissension in the house of any kind always upsets me. I'm hoping that peace will be restored soon and I'm
doing what I can—not much—to promote it.

It's a beautiful day here, after a week of dark rainy weather. The
pansies I planted in a box on the stoop look awful. Maybe today
will give them strength if not hope, which inhabitants of Upstate
New York know better than to entertain. I will move a couple of big
flourishing geraniums outdoors today but will wait to move my hi-
biscus, which is seven feet high and has six blossoms on it. It looms
over my table in the workroom, giving me the illusion of working in
the woods all winter.

Much love, as ever, HC

June 26, 1994

Dear Jane,

Feeding the dog her breakfast has become a pleasant ritual. I wash out her dish, dry it, put in the food, sprinkle brewer's yeast on top—against the fleas, but for her it's a delicacy as well—and give her fresh water, while she stands wagging her tail and making little eager noises in her throat. This morning, however, when I set her dishes on the floor she went and got her ball, and dropped it at my feet, the way she does when she wants to entice me into a game. "Stacey, you're a strange and foolish dog," I said. "You'd rather play than eat." But then I began to see that in fact she was trying to thank me in the only way she can. She "assumes" that if playing ball gives her so much pleasure it must give everyone else pleasure too. She wanted to do something for me in return for her breakfast, and she can't imagine that I find the ball boring as hell. Which casts a new light on our relationship. When I out of a sense of obligation play with her and throw the ball for her to fetch and worry, she thinks (perhaps) that she's entertaining me, fulfilling her appointed role. We are both creatures of duty. I'm not sure if I like that myself. But clearly she does.

Love, HC

PATRICK DONNELLY
The Charge (2003)

Patrick Donnelly is an Associate Editor at Four Way Books, and has taught at Colby College and the Bread Loaf Writers' Conference. *The Charge* is his first book. His writing has appeared in *American Poetry Review, Ploughshares, The Yale Review, The Virginia Quarterly Review,* and *The Massachusetts Review.* He had completed a new book of poems, and is working on translations of Japanese poetry and drama with Stephen Miller, to whom he is married.

In his own words: "I wrote *The Charge* as a time-capsule letter to the future, a lyric record of how it felt when some survived a dangerous time and some did not. Often when I read the Hebrew psalms in the great King James translation, I think: 'There's something familiar about that voice, how he wobbles between self-deprecating praise of the Beloved and a shamelessly subjective tantrum of longing.' Then I remember, 'Oh wait, that's me; I'm that guy.' If I imagine any future reader might have a similar thought about a poem I wrote, it makes me deeply happy. Not merely to fulfill my selfish desire: but may the tribe survive."

FOUNTAIN OF BLOOD

Les grands jets d'eau sveltes parmi les marbres

Sometime last week, in my neighbor's yard,
whoever it was, with whatever tool, broke up the concrete,
arranged the shattered slag around an oval of soil
that last looked at light and drank rain circa 1894,
and plunged a plant into that barely-breathing dirt.

I hate to say just *plant*, I've known men and women less alive
than this ornamental grass—"ornamental" a slander
unless a tiger is an ornament, a leaping zebra,
a striped fountain of blood, a great grass-gush seven feet tall
jetting panicles like foxtails over the fence, soft to the touch,
weeping rye, oats, millet, wheat, bread and the broken host of love
to the pavement, to be licked up by deertongue
and the ghosts of our long lost Brooklyn sheep and stock.

How will it live, in these ruins? How will I?

PRAYER AT THE OPERA

I had already been weeping quietly
for half an hour at the Academy of Music
by the time Ulysses finally made it home
disguised as a beggar. He was begging
for his son to recognize him, to *know* him,
and the boy longed to, but a whole kingdom
hung on this, and he was afraid to love a fraud.

When the Croatian baritone
stretched out his hand to the boy,
quivering thin and lonely
on the other side of the stage,
and sung his name softly,
Telemaco, Telemaco, mio diletto,
it was as if the floor of the world
tilted the boy into his arms,

and because I thought I heard my father calling,
I thought all voices were my voice begging
You, who made it easy for me to weep:
lend the gift of tears
to a man my mother said cried two times,
when Kennedy was shot,
and at my birth.

PRAYER AFTER THE BATHS

Thank You
for causing no man to love me
for more than a few minutes at a time
with such art as big, tall Tom has used this night,

because when he took off his baseball cap
to rub his buzzcut along my belly,
murmuring under his breath a baritonal "Sweet,"
I was in danger of becoming one of those
who have their reward in *this* life,

and then the proud palm-shaded pew
You in Your famous jealousy
have prepared for me
among the ranks of minor martyrs
might have gone
unoccupied.

YOUNG MAN READING COLETTE ON THE TRAIN

You hold my gaze a little too long,
your hair cut short like a boy's,
your fine little glasses,
at your ear, glint of gold,
in your cheek, a slight shade of wasting:
This is to say I see you, I know you,
I am alert to your potential, to ours,
on this train, on every train,
on the platform, on the stairs to the street,
on the dim threshold, in the elevator
stopped between floors, in its flickering lights,
then in that dark opening, if we are spared,
where I may find my way
to you, graceful ghost of a chance.

PRAYER AFTER REFUSING TO PRAY

Why, when the ferocious beauty that steers this world
has never braked for any cry of mine,

do I find myself making again, toward You
who will always do just as You please,

these motions with my lips and hands and knees,
trying to gentle Your vast wheel off the rails?

My friend is sick in the lymph behind his heart,
a monk, a teacher, Your servant, who loved You so.

CONSUMMATUM EST

With the certainty theologians claim
for the salvation worked by Christ—
effects not yet seen,
but the end not in doubt—
some women look back and know
the exact moment they conceived.

He brought me home from the baths
and fed me takeout Chinese. I remember
succulent little bits of egg in rice,
creamy sherbet right out of the carton.
Yes—certainly I felt it—and broke
into a sweat, the exact moment
the charge leapt from him to me.

Was it two years later his best friend called—
could I use his clothes, his shoes, his king-size bed?

PRAYER AT THE GYM

Only an All-Powerful Name
invoked again and again
gives me victory
over middle age, a chronic virus,
the disinclination to lift these weights,
and the crevice between my eyes
reflected to me from mirrors that are everywhere
mocking the idea that my body can be beautiful in this life.

But I'm shocked to discover,
looking up from my hundredth whispered *Bismillah,*
I'm not the only one praying here:
the brute on the fly machine
with the black bandana over his shaved skull—
R.I.P. WOLFMAN SHORTY inked by hand
on his right biceps, Twin Towers on the left,
his sexy little belly, if I read right, that says
he's caught the kitty too (from shooting up,
my guess, and not like me, from men)—
as he inserts the weight pin at 150
murmurs "Just one more,"
crosses himself, kisses
something he holds in his right hand,
then touches the weights in front of his heart
with a tremendous spasm of will—
      Oh God
help us to lift it
and go on lifting it,
the heavy burden of Your light.

HOW THE AGE OF IRON
TURNED TO GOLD

My death makes her way to me
carrying green leaves.

I hear my prayer coming
behind illness, romantic noise,

urgent telephone messages,
alchemical lab results,

like a brook weaving
through thicket.

Water knows the way,
it isn't lost.

My teacher comes to me
by the western gates,

her eyes gone violet
as the peal of a bell

as she bends to gather
all her tender puppies by the neck.

INSTANT COFFEE

When every winged thing
was falling for sweetness
        in my cup,
in the last dregs of light
at the end of a sunset dock,
        I gave up
and poured it in the lake,
and watched that cloud of cream
        expand and hold
an instant in the dark water,
before summer knelt
        into the cold,
dispersing her bright crystals.

LILAH HEGNAUER
Dark Under Kiganda Stars (2005)

Lilah Hegnauer's *Dark Under Kiganda Stars* was an honorable mention for the 2007 Library of Virginia Literary Award. She received an MFA from the University of Virginia and her poems have been published in *FIELD, Agni, Kenyon Review, Orion, The Drunken Boat,* and *So to Speak.* She is a recipient of an Astraea Lesbian Writers Grant and lives in Charlottesville, Virginia.

In her own words: *"Dark Under Kiganda Stars* is based on my time spent teaching English in Uganda during 2003. Its primary focus was to explore the intersection between teaching and writing, self and others, or identity and communication. What are the limits to communicating with others? How do we experience otherness and individuality? What is the role of the poet in terms of witness and how do we negotiate the boundary between witness and exploitation? In *Dark Under Kiganda Stars,* I respond viscerally to my particular experiences of teaching, loving, and otherness in Uganda."

TEACH ANYTHING

Teach anything, the headmaster told me;
he didn't return for five weeks. Clueless
as a gift chicken, I slowly learned
our lessons: they didn't know about

the slave trade, Martin Luther King, snow,
informal greetings, Shakespeare. Everything
was new, the world of English burst forth
tart on their palates: verbs, nouns,

conjugation of tenses. Amanyire whispered
to Mukabalisa, "Whatever you choose to claim
of me is always yours, *nkwagala*;" I dropped
my jaw. My hands and their papers dropped.

English infiltrated their romance. I can't
understand my body turning toward them,
turning away, turning again, and finally away;
English, Luganda, they're speaking Luzungu.

I learn each evening, roasting maize on charcoal,
language doesn't matter when it comes to love.
Like yellow kernels taking on the heat,
gradually we all want to be printed upon.

If I could sink myself into this ink and write myself
onto a page I would lie down in what they taught me
about iambs: walk under a full moon to the latrine—don't
light the lantern, leave it next to the sleeper.

Go later in the month when the moon is a hair, don't
light the lantern, fumble to the pit and back into bed.
Teach anything. Print the way upon your mind
until it's all sensory, all footpath-thin, all charted loam.

I THOUGHT SHE WAS SINGING

I looked out the window, I thought
she was singing. Three women,
one large in the middle, two thin
on the sides, nearly to the edge

of the dispensary land, and the
middle woman sank to a deep squat.
One baby tore out with its large head;
she was ashen, armless, still.

The women sang, lowering the mother
fully to the ground, laying her back
on the grass, and curling her knees
onto her belly. A smaller baby pushed

against her bones; out of nowhere
her legs shot up, soles to sky.
Our midwife pushed her hand
into the woman as the child tried to slip

cord first into the world. She pushed
the baby into the mother and slid the cord
in front of her face, down her tiny body.
How did she pull her hand out again

and quickly catch this small twin
swimming out face down? The midwife
wrapped her pink body in the mother's
travelling cloth like ears of roasted maize.

Oh—their singing—from the body,
of the body—is not simple.
The large, full song is the body is
wailing and singing—those who have not

known the extremes of both pains
can never understand the difference.
I looked out the window at
four women, two infants, one placenta

aching out right here, right between
the dispensary and convent.
Those who know extremes, can never
fully love those of us who are ignorant.

CHEWING

I.
In the beginning, the meat was tender,
flavored with chili powder, salt; as the
weeks passed, the meat grew tough;
chewing, I would finds bits of
bone and gristle. "Take more hard meat,"
you said at lunch, "always take more,
always more to be taken."

II.
On the back of the motorcycle, sidesaddle
as you drove to market, you asked,
"are you secure?" and the word came out
se-chewer. Yes, hooking my fingers
around your hip bones, thumbs through
your belt, twisting my torso so my breasts
leaned square into your shoulder blades,
I was ready when the bike climbed gears.

III.
Before cooking the dinner beef,
a cutting from the same old cow,
you kneaded coarse salt, pushing
into its rawness with the palms
of your hands, trying to soften
its fibers. Trying to keep me
from looking at your bleeding hand
you asked, "I'm curious, how is Fildah?"
and the word came out chew-rious.

IV.
Your hand bled into the meat,
the meat bled into the wooden board,
and after dinner, while everyone slept,
we continued chewing. The vestiges
of your salty palm blood pressed into
my temples as we sang psalms
in the farthest garden. You claimed
you could hear me through your hands,
so I sang in my body through your palms.

DARK UNDER KIGANDA STARS

Dark under Kiganda stars, the night dove was calling
when Arlene came home feverish with the flu.
That was the night you rubbed antiseptic balm
to coat the inside of my nose and ears and she put
ginger in her porridge and chewed the pork bones after dinner.
Dark under Kiganda stars, the night dove was calling
when I pressed your pink shirt and burned my arm
swinging the charcoal iron to heat it up again.
That was the night I discovered endearments
in English directly translated from Luganda—
I was a lion with hair of molten lava.
Dark under Kiganda stars, the night dove was calling
and I saw your eyes open slowly after sleeping
with the rhythm of a slow procession drum;
that was the night they also opened quickly,
like a startled chicken beating its wings
from chest to sky, when I kicked the tin of shoe polish.
Dark under Kiganda stars, the night dove was calling
when your eyes didn't blink and, pink tongue between
white teeth between brown lips, you whispered, "I'm so black."
That was the night you tried to remember
the passage from Kunitz's "King of the River"
'I did not choose the way, the way chose me'.
Dark under Kiganda stars, the night dove was calling
when you stumbled and asked me to practice
Luganda—Nkwagala. Sula bulungi
That was the night we listened to the rain make mud.

PROVERB XII: THE HUNTER

The hunter in search
of an elephant
does not stop to throw
stones at birds.
It seems we don't hunt,
though, and the elephants
are long gone from this place.
The name of the hill,
Mpologoma, means lions,
but there are none; there is
no one left who remembers
the name as accurate. Your
mother away at a meeting
with the women of the
parish, you and I and the
black goat wandered out
in the pasture, past the
cows chewing in their sleep.
Out farther and farther,
almost to the house of the
muzeyi who celebrated her
hundred and third feast day
last week. I was so weary
with heat and chalk and
papers to mark, we
stopped at the edge of the pasture
and sank to the earth.
Sometime, this will all

come back to me, I fear.
There was no elephant,
there was no hunt, there
were only tinkerbirds,
palm swifts and the black goat
trilling and bleating; here
and there a honeyguide
puffed its yellow cheekfeathers
with air and sound and song—
more song, I fear, than I'll ever remember.

TUNG-HUI HU
Mine (2007)

Tung-Hui Hu writes on film and new media in San Francisco. He is the author of two collections of poetry, *Mine* (2007) and *The Book of Motion* (2003), and has held residencies at MacDowell Colony and the University of Mississippi.

In his own words: "I'm interested in how we claim a landscape as 'ours' or 'mine,' and in the way real persons and landscapes push up against fictionalized versions of them. I live in an American West haunted by but also settled through stories of gold miners, railroads, orange trees. The actual stories are less important than the voice with which we tell them: the patterns in speech that invoke a sense of belonging."

THE WISH ANSWERED

Several years ago I discovered
how easily love and food are confused,
when I thought I was in love with someone
but really it was a skipped lunch,
forgive me, I was young,
passions being what they were
were somewhat equivalent, mixed-up,
the highest anything,
stars without firmament, colors huddled
in the back shelf of a dark closet.
And even when I got my wish,
her sitting in front of me,
all I could think about
was cannoli, biscotti.
How embarrassing! My stomach
growled and my heart leapt.

FIVE DOLLARS

She tells you to bring her five dollars. You go home. You look for change in the couch. You bring it to her. She turns off the light. You lie in the dark with your clothes off. Nobody moves. You have seen geese stunned after flying into a glass window: it is the same thing with your bodies. You hope something will change color. You hope it is something uprooted inside of you. You start to worry someone will find you still there the next morning. Your neck is beginning to get sore. You say Is that it? She says Yeah, that's what it is. The lights go on. You look down. It is the dew that appears after a summer night.

INSTRUCTIONS RECEIVED BY NEW COLONY

One soldier's rifle at my back:
for a minute we walked
like this, his barrel, my shirt,
I leading the way, a brother
showing a brother where
to eat, where to hide. Nothing
was wrong the night of Easter,
only this bell calling us
down from the hillside,
its throat saying metal-for-
heartbeats, rise-and-fall-of-the-day,
hope is lost, war is won, orange
trees and candlewax burning.

Here is what the soldier thought:
the footraces when we were young—
people would slow down to scoop
up the yellow apples we would
toss, crisp as a bell ringing.
No, it was more like this:
after the hunt the air is
heavy with birds and frogs,
their lungs inflating like a bell
set loose in the ocean.

*

Go, then, to the place where they still sew with
needles of boar bristle, and build your
city there. How boars are caught:
in the trees, some men chase, others run,
imitating pheasants.

*

You were burned once by their rope
that sang like a bird. You clung to it
like a boy holding a blade of grass.

Now they give you mud walls and spaces
between rocks, arms of trees outstretched
to point the way skywards, weeds and weeds
for health. They give you cities of
ladders and ramparts. When you see

a woman appear you stay there,
this woman (Kore you call her) of rope
that is to say with feet tied together
you bury her.

*

Not that way.

*

Like you, I hated running
from country to country, each
place the same people, just
uglier, older, as if a
gigantic hand had pressed hard
against their faces, fusing
together bones, leaving some
cross-eyed, color-blind. And yet
in the plains we can feel
the lake rising at our backs,
steamships that cross when fog sets
over the cornstalks, the sight
of pumpkins and squash splayed
on vines like exposed ovaries,
bumps and all, orange, green.
When our neighbor gave us zucchini,
we tried for a week to get rid
of it, zucchini in bread,
zucchini in applesauce,
zucchini in pies, and what
we think he was saying was
simple: Vines, not people,
follow you everywhere you go.

from AND ABOUT TIME

In purity you have removed everything
from your room & as a canyon holds a bridge
in its arms your body stretches
across morning. With eyes
closed or open it is the same,
sheets and walls and summer sky.
Soon you will smell the cigar
smoke from the courtyard so that
even the palm leaves are dripping

in it, you will walk
to the sink to wash your hands
of the blood you have accumulated
igneous as basalt. And you will say
to us I am so beautiful I am
the meridian between the days.

*

There are three notes in this song I can stand
and the rest just scaffolding like the white

moat that surrounds a wound.
Listen, here are the things I will not

speak to you about because then I'd have nothing left:

a maple bench, smooth to the touch. Glenn Gould singing
in the background of his recordings.
The ability to jerk your hand
out of harm's

way: say from a hot stove. And slats of light
through the shutters.

*

When we are very rich (so rich that
the gilt on sunlight belongs to us) we will
say to ourselves: "And about time." And
there will have been no gap between

when we first desired and when we got.
So this is to fill in all those
moments in between,
those you will have no memory of—

once when everything was wrong
you (stronger than daybreak) tore
apart the living room. Splinters
and plant soil on the floor.

And when it was over
you arose, thinking There will be hell to pay.

Nobody said a thing
and this knowledge has hurt you
more than anything else.

from THE RIVER

It is true that you, Cecilia/Natalie, act differently: you've started eating the fish that we catch. No—there is no need, the fish here are small and bony, more like jewels than food. And your eyes shine yellow now at night, like a cat's. You once told me about a dream you had: floating in the salt water, face down, tasting fish as the schools swim past. No brassière. You've eaten so many fish you worry you'll sink, you worry you'll spend years at the bottom waiting for someone to find you, to kiss you, to cut open your stomach—only then will the rubies and sapphires tumble out and let you float again.

LINTON KWESI JOHNSON
Mi Revalueshanary Fren (2006)

Linton Kwesi Johnson is the most influential black poet in Britain. The author of five previous collections of poetry and numerous record albums, he is known world-wide for his fusion of lyrical verse and reggae. Though he has lived in England since the age of twelve, much of his verse is written in the Jamaican Creole of his homeland, and he considers his early childhood years to have had a great influence on his work. He was only the second living poet in history to be published in Penguin's distinguished Modern Classics series. *Mi Revalueshanary Fren* is his first U.S. publication.

In his own words: "The faculty of the creative imagination is a defining characteristic of what it means to be human. Art provides us with mirrors through which we can see ourselves, not only as we are, but also offers us visions of how we could be. Art not only reflects reality, it allows us to transcend and transform reality. We socialise through art in pursuit of leisure and pleasure and art can provide us with fleeting and occasionally enduring insights into the human condition. Art is also an active agent in our psychological equilibrium as a means of personal and social catharsis. And art is a crucial factor in the formation of identities. Art as commodity provides people with jobs. Art is central to our spiritual well-being too." —from an interview in *New Statesman*.

REALITY POEM

dis is di age af reality
but some a wi a deal wid mitalagy
dis is di age af science an teknalagy
but some a wi a check fi antiquity

wen wi can't face reality
wi leggo wi clarity
some latch awn to vanity
some hol insanity
some get vizshan
start preach relijan
but dem can't mek decishan
wen it come to wi fite
dem can't mek decishan
wen it come to wi rites

man,
dis is di age af reality
but some a wi a deal wid mitalagy
dis is di age af science an teknalagy
but some a wi a check fi antiquity

dem one deh gaan outta line
dem naw live in fi wi time
far dem seh dem get sign
an dem bline dem eye
to di lite a di worl
an gaan search widin
di dark a dem doom
an a shout bout sin
instead a fite fi win

man,
dis is di age af reality
but some a wi a deal wid mitalagy
dis is di age af science an teknalagy
but some a wi a check fi antiquity

dis is di age af decishan
soh mek wi leggo relijan
dis is di age af decishan
soh mek wi leggo divishan
dis is di age af reality
soh mek wi leggo mitalagy
dis is di age af science an teknalagy
mek wi hol di clarity
mek wi hol di clarity

INGLAN IS A BITCH

wen mi jus come to Landan toun
mi use to work pan di andahgroun
but workin pan di andahgroun
yu dont get fi know your way aroun

Inglan is a bitch
dere's no escapin it
Inglan is a bitch
dere's no runin whe fram it

mi get a likkle jab in a big otell
an awftah a while, mi woz doin quite well
dem staat mi awf as a dish-washah
but wen mi tek a stack, mi noh tun clack-watchah!

Inglan is a bitch
dere's no escapin it
Inglan is a bitch
noh baddah try fi hide fram it

wen dem gi you di likkle wage packit
fus dem rab it wid dem big tax rackit
yu haffi struggle fi mek enz meet
an wen yu goh a yu bed yu jus cant sleep

Inglan is a bitch
dere's no escapin it
Inglan is a bitch fi true
a noh lie mi a tell, a true

me use to work dig ditch wen it cowl noh bitch
mi did strang like a mule, but, bwoy, mi did fool
den awftah a while mi jus stap dhu owevahtime
den awftah a while mi jus phu dung mi tool

Inglan is a bitch
dere's no escapin it
Inglan is a bitch
yu haffi know how fi suvive in it

well mi dhu day wok an mi dhu nite wok
mi dhu clean wok and mi dhu dutty wok
dem seh dat black man is very lazy
but if yu si how mi wok yu woodah seh mi crazy

Inglan is a bitch
dere's no escapin it
Inglan is a bitch
yu bettah face up to it

dem have a likkle facktri up inna Brackly
inna disya facktri all dem dhu is pack crackry
fi di laas fifteen years dem get mi laybah
now awftah fifteen years mi fall out a fayvah

Inglan is a bitch
dere's no escapin it
Inglan is a bitch
dere's no runin whe fram it

mi know dem have wok, wok in abundant
yet still, dem mek mi redundant
now, at fifty-five mi getin quite ole
yet still, dem sen mi fi goh draw dole

Inglan is a bitch
dere's no escapin it
Inglan is a bitch fi true
is whe wi a goh dhu bout it?

YOUT SCENE

last satdey
I nevah deh pan no faam,
so I decide fi tek a walk
doun a Brixton
an see wha gwaan.

di bredrin dem stan-up
outside a Hip City,
as usual, a look pretty;
dem a lawf big lawf
dem a talk dread talk
dem a shuv an shuffle dem feet,
soakin in di sweet musical beat.

but when nite come
policeman run dem dung;
beat dem dung a grung,
kick dem ass,
sen dem paas justice
to prison walls of gloom.

but di breddah dem a scank;
dem naw rab bank;
is pakit dem a pick
an is woman dem a lick
an is run dem a run when di wicked come.

SONG OF BLOOD

I trod di day
all di way
an ride di nite
clutchin site
movin sway
searchin lite ...

there's a glow on the hill, way over yonder
there's the blast of the guns down below

I screw di sun
jus fi fun
paint di moon blue
spiritually true
mystically spun
perpetually new ...

there are robbers in the gullies, on the streets
there are wicked men sitting in the seats of judgement

I check di stars
all di scars
dat wound an heal
di dread I feel
di dread I star
di dark I seal ...

there's a sign in the flash that slashes the nite
there's the sound of the drums poundin blood gushin down

I hurt di pain
again an again
hole di sting
an mek it sing
an mek it pain
an mek it ring . . .

there are sufferers with guns movin breeze through the trees
there are people waging war in the heat and hunger of the streets.

SEASONS OF THE HEART

Beguiled
by blue moon
O enchanting light

we lost our way
like lovers sometime do
searching wide-eyed
for wild flowers
in the "fragrant forest of the night"

now memories
slowly drift on by
like grey clouds
against a sombre winter sky
and all our yesterdays are now become
the springtime of our days

life is the greatest teacher
love is the lesson to be learnt
like how the heart's seasons shift
how the sweet smelling blossoms of spring
are soon become the icy arrows of winter's sting
how spring intoxicated by the sun
now throws off her green gown
and summer's golden smile is soon become
the frown of autumn's brown
how passion spent we droop like sapless vines
in the winter of our minds

LAURA KASISCHKE
Gardening in the Dark (2004)
Lilies Without (2007)

Laura Kasischke is the author of seven books of poetry, including *Lilies Without, Gardening in the Dark, Dance and Disappear* (Juniper Prize, 2002), and four novels. Her work has received many honors, including the Alice Fay diCastagnola Award from the Poetry Society of America, the Beatrice Hawley Award, the Pushcart Prize, and the Elmer Holmes Bobst Award for Emerging Writers. She teaches at the University of Michigan in Ann Arbor.

In her own words: "I realized while ordering and selecting the poems for this collection that much of my more recent work concerns body parts, dresses, and beauty queens. These weren't conscious decisions, just the things that found their ways into my poems at this particular point in my life, and which seem to have attached to them a kind of prophetic potential. The beauty queens especially seemed to crowd in on me, in all their feminine loveliness and distress, wearing their physical and psychological finery, bearing what body parts had been allotted to them. For some time, I had been thinking about beauty queens like Miss Michigan, but also the Rhubarb Queen, and then Beauty Queens of abstraction—congeniality. And then—Brevity, Consolation for Emotional Damages, Estrogen—all these feminine possibilities to which I thought a voice needed to be given."

NEW DRESS

Dress of dreams and portents, worn

in memory, despite
the posted warnings
sunk deeply into the damp
sand
all along the shore. (*The green*

tragedy of the sea
about to happen to me.) Even

in my subconscious, I ignored them.
(*The green*

eternity of the sea, just around the corner.) That

whole ominous summer, I wore it, just
an intimation
then, a bit
of threatening ephemera. Another
rumor. Another
vicious whisper. And then
they sang. (*The giddy*

green
girls
of the sea.)

The feminine

maelstrom
of it, I wore. (*How*

quiet, at the edge of it, the riot. How

tiny, the police.) The *Sturm*

und Drang of it. The crypt
and mystery. The knife
in fog of it. The haunted
city of my enemy.
(*And always*
the green, floating, open
book of the sea.) That

dress, like

an era of deafness and imminent error, ending
even as I wore it, even as I dragged the damp

hem of it
everywhere
I wore it.

MISS CONGENIALITY

There's a name given
after your death
and a name you must answer to while you're alive.

Like flowers, my friends—nodding, nodding. My
enemies, like space, drifting
away. They

praised my face, my enunciation, the power
I freely relinquished, and the fires

burning in the basements of my churches,
and the pendulums swinging
above my towers.
And my

heart (which was a Boy Scout

lost for years in a forest.) And my

soul (although the judges said
it weighed almost nothing
for goodness had devoured it.)

They praised my feet, the shoes
on my feet, my feet
on the floor, the floor—
and then

144

the sense of despair
I evoked with my smile, the song

I sang. The speech
I gave

about peace, in praise of the war. O,

they could not grant me the title I wanted

so they gave me the title I bore,

and stubbornly refused
to believe I was dead
long after my bloody mattress
had washed up on the shore.

THE THIGH

Clothing and weapons set aside, I am simply your thigh, and proof
that underneath the world lies
a warm pool of water overflowing
with drowned blue butterflies.

All these years,
clear up to here:
As you waited, I waited too.
When you were tired,
I lay down with you.
You never noticed,
but now you do. (*That
boy's fingers whispering past the hem of your skirt—guess who?*)

Guess who.

Sleeve of moony, vaporous voices. The dead ebbing as the living
       flowed.
The calm milked cows in a field of clover. The long
white fish in a bath. Cellular
shadow on the forest floor. Someone withdraws
a shining sword.
The naked man standing on the deck with his harpoon.
So much water lapping at a mindless shore. So
much spring stuffed into a pale
silk sack.
Or a club

tossed down among the flowers.

I am your memory
of it all, your life, in flesh and hours, statement
and tone, meat and weather

wrapped around a bone.

WAR WITH TOY SOLDIERS

They have fallen off the coffee table
onto the floor. They have slipped
under rugs, lost
their guns, found

themselves in the strange
gray dream between
the floral cushions and the upholstery. They

have been batted all over the house by the cat, dropped
their canteens
down the register grates, forgotten

their homelands, their languages, their names. They

have fallen out of love.
Boarded the wrong trains.
Laughed loud and long late into the night
while digging their own graves. They

have bathed in rain. Trudged through mud. Been
drunk. Driven

in long convoys of trucks without brakes across desert plains.

They have stood at the edges
of swiftly moving rivers, watching

time flounder down to the ocean, singing,
Once, there was not even a plan.
A plan still had to be made.

Now, it's Monday. September.
The children have vanished
from the dream of their summer vacation, and

a mother, on her knees, alone
in the house for the first time in months
could assess this situation, could see

how the pure white deer that always wanders

onto the battlefield
after the violence

stands now at the center
of the wonder in silence.

GARY COPELAND LILLEY
Alpha Zulu (2008)

Gary Copeland Lilley is a graduate of the Warren Wilson College MFA Program, and lives, drums, and writes in the Asheville, NC area.

In his own words: "I write because I don't know how to not write. It is such a part, integral part, of my life that if I am not putting written words together, revising, or researching a project something is askew. The last time that happened was during my submarine service. But I was just as aware that I was not writing as I was conscious of our submerged depth. At the time I liked being on a submarine, seeing everything under pressure, sometimes ahead full outside the safe operating envelope. I guess that's my approach to poetry, too. I have lived most my life in marginalized communities where I find, in addition to the pressure, substance, beauty, and art everywhere I look. I'm vigilant, I can't help it, I observe people. This writing thing is what I do."

ALPHA ZULU

I know more people dead than people alive,
my insomniac answer to self-addressed prayers

is that in the small hours even God drinks alone.
My self-portrait: gray locks in the beard, red eyes

burning back in the mirror, the truths of grooves
and nicks on my face, one missing tooth.

I'm a man who's gathered too many addresses,
too many goodbyes. There's not much money

or time left to keep on subtracting from my life.
Except for needs I can pack everything I have

into my old black sea-bag. *To all the bloods*
I'll raise a bourbon, plant my elbow on the bar

and drink to the odds that one more shot
won't have me wearing a suit of blues.

I'm so exposed, with you all of me is at risk,
and if that's only one side of being in love

that's the one deep down that proves it.
Here you are sleeping with me, narcotic as night,

naked as an open hand, and the skinny of it is,
what makes you think I am afraid of this

when I once lived in a cave, moss on the cold wall,
all my bones scattered across the floor.

STILL LIFE WITH DOME LIGHT

Look at them glowing around the payphone
by Abraham's store, like three chicken wings
with mumbo sauce, ghosting like stolen cars
with busted back windows and broken lights,
yesterday's newspapers being resold,
dark spaces inside a tattoo parlor.
I know that they've spotted me, nobody's
going to touch a stash until I'm gone.
Makes me want to spread their cheeks on the curb,
hands interlocked on top of doo-ragged heads,
all the custom-fitted ball caps tossed in
the storm drain. Into the piss stank down-flow
where they should be. I want to hold them there
all night, while crackheads stumble up and leave.

THE MARY MAGDALENE CEREMONY

It's the first moment, the touch of water
when an addicted woman can forget.
She is no longer sick at the sink

between street and towel in the bathroom,
but in green hills where she hears one crow
calling sun to the tree. A cool air moves

the bush, all the secrets of crevices
and rocks are exposed. The water running,
she splashes a hand into the valley,

the misdemeanors and felonies fall
into the mirrored lake and what remains
is offered, a blessed less than perfect light.

WAHTUH

A summer storm shot across my luck,
the machine voice, the flat palm of a woman
on weed, motor oil, and persistent rumors.
To cool my ear I'll need a river.
Such a mean sky, a dizzy lick,
a thrill-time garden of ricochets,
that ecstatic carnival urge, her gracious giggle
when we leave the road through a tunnel of trees
on Johns Island, South Carolina.
Longing to be a good night tingle lizard
hitting thermal shots straight up,
I drive through her rain and mud
then we're holding close on a porch rocker,
she's back and forth, calling me in the Gullah.

THE DEEP DIVE EPISTLE
OF WATCH SECTION 3

Lester Yates, your blow-up doll
should have stayed in port.
We are tired of seeing your date
in front of the scheduled flick,
and sitting in the crew's mess
when we're eating chow.
The gapped washable mouth
and her insensitive green eyes
deaden every fantasy in our heads.
We have taken and deflated her.
If you expect to see your friend again
you will do exactly as we say.
If you buck against anything
we'll send you her limp left leg.
You are to get 3 packs of cigarettes,
one of which will be menthol,
and one unfiltered. Leave them all
by the anchor housed indicator
and then walk the submarine
from torpedo tubes, aft, through control,
missile mid-level, past the reactor
and into the heat of the engine room.
Wait at the shaft wearing nothing
but skivvies and a dosimeter.
Try not to sweat into the deck
and we will contact you there
with further instructions.

BONEMAN

Don't care who they are
I get paid good to do this
smash the slugger first
against the right hand
and disregard their scream
wait that long moment
then proceed to work
the opposite side both arms
below the elbow my God
you can almost see them
think this is going to be all
and then the left foot I hit it
above the arch my one bit
of mercy I leave the ankle
that's begging for attention
the snap stick bone of the leg
under the knee the shock
by that time usually shuts
the mouth the muscles
of the thigh make a clean
break difficult so I bring
the john henry hard.

UNMARKED GRAVE

Old man, if it'll help you rest, the shotgun
that has gone from first son to first son

did not come to me, but I do wear the epitaph
of one of your old suits. I remember we stood

in the order of our birth years, children
of the children you left, all holidays

waiting the big Buick to pull in the yard.
For those meals of ash, now you have no stone.

I remember how much you drank and cussed.
Pistol, you burned your people like a torch.

A weed stalk is the devil's walking stick,
the bastard, I know it matters to you

that none of your blood will bring a flower
and nobody but me will cut this grass.

ERZU-LEE ENTERS
MUSTANG SALLY'S DRAG BAR

The sharpest knife in the drawer
can't cut a deck no deeper than her.

Blessed queen of hearts in pearls and jeans,
hoop earrings, a bracelet of tattoos,

a blouse you can almost see through
and those stripper shoes. A sweet water flows

across the floor and banks against a gambler's leg.
The luck struck player clears his throat,

hides his next card in the hole,
parks his red deuce and a quarter in the pot,

tells the sweet girl to come sit by his side
and to order any drink she wants.

GATESVILLE, JOE SEARS' PLACE

Where every wail and whoop
raises up roadhouse dust
and the one-arm proprietor
skins a smile and cuts a thick cigar
on the real teeth side of his mouth
expertly turning
his pistol hip away from the bar
pouring liquor fast
not spilling a drop and keeping
his bloodshot eye
on everyone.

KHALED MATTAWA

Zodiac of Echoes (2003)
Amorisco (2008)

Khaled Mattawa was born in Libya, and immigrated to the US in his teens. The author of *Ismailia Eclipse* and *Zodiac of Echoes* (poems), and translator of three volumes of contemporary Arabic poetry, he has received the Alfred Hodder Fellowship at Princeton University, a Guggenheim Fellowship, and a National Endowment for the Arts translation grant. He teaches at the University of Michigan in Ann Arbor.

In his own words: "Amorisco is a nonce word that combines the Spanish 'amor' and 'Morisco.' Moriscos were Iberian Muslims (Moors) who in the 15th to the 17th centuries were given the choice to convert to Catholicism or leave Iberia. Most were expelled by the decree of 1610 from Spain to North Africa after being persecuted by the Spanish Inquisition. Inspired by that historical juncture and its metaphorical suggestions, *Amorisco* is above all a formal challenge. Some of the poem are lyrics of twenty lines or shorter, inspired by the distillation and conceptual density of Antonio Machado, Saadi Youssef, and Rainer Maria Rilke. I wanted to write in that pure mode that seems to transcend time and circumstance, and that in many cases acts as a skeleton upon which much of poetry is placed. In the longer poems that range freely among pressing questions and unresolved episodes I work in counter-mode attaching, welding, and knotting as much material (and prose) to a lyric impulse as it could handle. Of course, I love the lyric mode, but I sometimes resist its taciturn wisdom and the purity of its bones. So in the case of *Amorisco*, I try to challenge it by keeping the kinds of materials lyric excises, but that remain vital and relevant nonetheless."

CORPUS CHRISTI

Your head buzzing with Lorca, flashbacks
of Almodovar drowning scenes—still,
I don't know why you went to Spain.
An archeological dig or business school?
Someone sent white roses, no note. In the yard,
I aimed the shotgun, then a drizzle of petals,
snow, cocaine. Your cat eats in the same corner; now
catches her own squirrels. There's a book about you,
all the little scandals you bragged about at parties—
the Polaroids of you and the mayor and his wife
sprawled nude on the traffic court bench.
Or your two trained pigs squealing the National Anthem
while you romped in a playground sand box.
I told them nothing about the baby iguanas
your father stole from the zoo, greased and baked,
nothing about the tufts of hair we yanked off
old ladies we abducted for ransom, or the peanut butter
jars filled with gnashed teeth. The last time
you called, the line was static and your voice
felt like hydrogen peroxide in my ear.
I sent 22 telegrams and you didn't answer. Now,
I drive to Lubbock on weekends. I think of you
among beat-up cars and broken glass, among
sawed-off guitars and hollow drums.
I think of the burlap jacket you made me,
the cheese cloth dresses you wore,
your mother's ashes, how you fed some
to your violets then poured the rest inside

a peppershaker in Houston's Hard Rock Café.
And the live wire across the street!
Birds tipped it for landing, the shock jerking them
back up, their screams short shrill gargles, then
on the sidewalk—two charred halves, the pile
of them you collected in the rear porch,
how stray dogs came barking at night,
how I clubbed two raccoons that broke the screen
and one left a scar on my calf. Love,
why can't we lie again on the sand,
chunks of cauliflower between our toes,
sunbathers gawking at us like they've always done,
and we weeping for their sake, because no one else would,
not the sky that's been clear for two years,
or the puny mist rising from the river, or the sea
doddering like a sloth? Let's leave now
and drive to the shady side of a plaza, watch
Mexican children run between gray and bronze,
fade in and out of a sun-scorched dream.

HEARTSONG

A bird sings from the tree. The birds sing
sending waves of desire and I stand on my roof
waiting for a randomness to storm my days. I stand
on my roof filled with the longing that sings its way
out of the bird. I am afraid that my call will break me,
that the cry blocked by my tongue will pronounce me mad.
O bird mad with longing, O balancing bar,
tight rope, monkey grunting from a roof. Fortunate bird.
I stand on my roof and wave centuries of desire.
I am the Bedouin pondering the abandoned campsite,
licking the ashes of the night fire; the American walking,
walking miles of dresses, blouses, and skirts filling them
with infinite lovers, the mystic feeling the pull swirling
in his chest, a desert of purpose expanding and burning
and yellowing every shade of green. And I stand on my roof.
And I say come like a stranger, like a feather
falling on an old woman's shoulder, like a hawk
that comes to feed from her hands, come like a mystery,
like sunlight rain, a blessing, a bus falling off a bridge,
come like a deserting soldier, a murderer chased by law,
like a girl prostitute escaping her pimp, come like a lost horse,
like a dog dying of thirst, come love, come ragged
and melancholy like the last day on earth, come like a sigh
from a sick man, come like a whisper, like a bump on the road,
like a flood, a dam breaking, turbines falling from the sky,
come love like the stench of a swamp, a barrage of light

filling a blind girl's eye, come like a memory convulsing
the body into sobs, like a carcass floating on a stream,
come like a vision, come love like a crushing need,
come like an afterthought. Heart song. Heart song.
The pole smashes and the live wires yellow streaks
on the lush grass. Come look and let me wonder. Someone.
So many. The sounds of footsteps, horses and cars.
Come look and let me wonder. I stand on my roof
echoing the bird's song: Do not sleep. Do not sleep now
that you have housed your longing within the pain of words.

EARLY ADULTHOOD

We made fires, outlined the conspiracies.
The scent of smoke lingered on our hands.

Straggling summer clouds, like newsless travelers,
gave the century the same name others gave theirs.

Some of us sent prayers skyward. Some slumped
in chairs, others sat up, their backs taut.

Does it matter who of these I was then
when under a clear sky all options were justified?

Yes, I thought of what I'd promised you.
But who was I then, or should I say what am I

in that place, or anywhere
and why, O why, does it keep changing?

Another language, another betrayal. The star
that once bloodied my grasp, a pinch of red dust.

ON THE MASTHEAD

Writing you from the sky again,
the plane a temple of strangers,
sleepers and insomniacs
needling the unwitting air.

I know you are the sea below,
the moon glow leavening the clouds.
I know you are the smoldering core,
the flame spluttering in eternal dark.

I know you are this journey.
You are separation and welding,
this suspension between eternity and dirt.

You are the love I carry with me,
my anger, my despair,
their atoms trailing from my heart.

You are sleep, the dream
that delights and terrorizes,
captivating, unrecountable.

You happen once and forever
like the air I breathe,
was and will be,
the I in you, the you in I.

I grasp you out of emptiness.
Hold fast to me,
dear little god.
I shall not let go of thee.

REDRESS

The relative who wronged you
you've already mistreated twice.
The friend who betrayed you—
and whom you betrayed—you've reconciled
since then, many kisses on the cheek.

The ex-lover who's badmouthed you
and you've badmouthed in return—
how blissful it'd be to be together again,
tracing scars you left on each other,
regret fueling your passionate sex.

This last thought pleases you as
you search for the proper pan,
the newly sharpened knife
that will slice up tonight's meal.
But what will you feed yourself?

Go wash your hands, go wash
your whole body. Let steam unstiffen
you, the foam drag away the rot.

And after you've combed your hair,
and rubbed sandalwood on your neck,
face the dark ground and kneel,
rest your forehead on the floor.

Say now the alkaline words of forgiveness,
and yes, go ahead and weep out the blows
you've received and recklessly thrown
until supplication is all that pegs you to life.

And when you rise, know that you are not
worthy of disdain or affection, but that
from now on you'll have to tighten your fists
on the last embers of love.

WILLIAM MATTHEWS
The Satires of Horace (Translations, 2002)

William Matthews, author of a dozen books of poetry, won the National Book Critics Circle Award for *Time & Money* in 1995, and, in 1997, the Ruth Lilly Award of the Modern Poetry Association. At the time of his death in 1997 he was Professor of English at the College of the City University of New York. Houghton Mifflin published *Search Party: Collected Poems of William Matthews*, in 2004.

In his own words: "Horace has written a great poem inviting a friend to dinner (Epistles I, 5). At the center of his imagination are things left out almost entirely from many a body of poetic work: friendship, pleasure, talk, food—much of what actually sustains us. For Horace, these subjects were not small, and he expended on them no less skill than Virgil needed to write his great epic.

Likewise, there's an interesting assumption about the audience in Horace's poems. 'Now if you ask me, what is it, Horace, you're driving at, here is my answer,' he'll write. There's a powerful fiction of conversation between equals in those poems. It sounds familiar to those of us in the Whitman line, as all American poets are: you invent an audience and speak to it—'Alone with America,' in Richard Howard's tolling phrase.

But of course Horace had a patron. He had had in fact *the* patron, Maecenas. Augustus read Horace's poems and found jokes in them. Horace could have written as if from an inner circle with no pretense. But his stance was inclusive, convivial, democratic. I suspect he was capable of deep depression, and that may have accounted some for Horace's invention of his audience of friendly equals, an adult version of a child's imaginary friend."

—interview with James Duffy in *New Hope for the Dead: Uncollected Matthews* (Red Hen Press, 2009).

SATIRE II, i

Horace: Some have complained my satires cut
such gashes I should fear libel suits, yet
others call them bloodless and insist satires
just as good could be cranked out a thousand
a day. Tell me, Trebatius, what should
I do? *Trebatius:* Take a break. *Horace:*
You mean write nothing at all? *Trebatius:* Just so.
Horace: Damn me if you're not right, but what then
will I do when I can't sleep? *Trebatius:* Slather
yourself with oil and swim in the Tiber back
and forth three times; then, after sunset
marinate yourself in wine. If you must
scribble, try some praise for our unvanquished
Caesar and blush on your way to the bank.
Horace: You're right, best of fathers, but I've not
got the skills I'd need to depict
lances bristling, dying Gauls with broken spears,
a skewered Parthian sliding slackly
from his horse. *Trebatius:* Then why not praise Caesar
for his just rule? Canny Lucilius
did that for Scipio. *Horace:* I'm ready
for that good luck when it's ready for me.
A Flaccus who hopes to pour a few words
in Caesar's ear needs to know when to tilt
his wrist. Curry that horse clumsily
and you'll feel a fusillade of hooves.
Trebatius: This is a better plan than writing
"Allswag, the parasite, and that spendthrift Nomentanus."

A line like that makes anyone think he
could be next, and through unscarred, he fears you.
Horace: Is it my fault that Milonius,
drunk on the fumes of his drunkenness, starts
seeing double and dances with himself?
Castor loves horses; Pollux, born from the same
egg, loves boxing. For every thousand souls
there are a thousand passions. I merely
capture this variety in meter, just
as Lucilius, a better man
than you or I. He confided to his books,
his faithful friends, and told his secrets nowhere else, in good times or worse.
So his work lets us view, as on a votive tablet,
the old poet's whole life. I follow his good
example. Whether I'm Apulian
or Lucanian, I don't know; settlers
in Venusia plowed close to borders
of both lands. Those settlers were sent to fill
the space the Samnites had been driven from,
or so the story goes, with this in mind:
to block a free path to Rome if either
the Lucanians or Apulians,
pugnacious races both, should threaten war.
But I'd not thrust my pen at anyone
who'd not provoked me. It's a defensive
weapon, like a sheathed sword. Why would I draw
it when I'm safe from thieves? O Jupiter,

Father and King, may my sword rust away
and no one harm me. Peace and quiet,
that's my ticket. "Hands off" is my motto:
anybody gives me any trouble, he'll be
swiftly famous for his pain and snuffling.
If you irk Cervius he'll yank you into court.
Canidia has poison concocted
by Albucius. If Terrius is judge
when you're in court, expect a savage fine.
We all have ways to ward off enemies,
by courtesy of Nature. Therefore wolves
fight with fangs and bulls with horns. Instinct taught
them how. Suppose prodigal Scaeva has
a long-lived mother. His pious hand
will not strike her. This isn't strange. A wolf
won't kick you, nor a bull bite. Some hemlock
in a honeysop will ease the old crone
into final sleep. Here's what I think: if long
age awaits me or death stretches out
its sable wings just now, rich or poor,
in Rome or in exile, whatever comes,
I can't not write. *Trebatius:* I fear a brief life
for you, young man. Some high-placed friends
of ours could chill you with a killing frost.
Horace: When Lucilius, first to compose
satires like this, peeled back the gleaming pelts
of some who strutted grandiosely
to show what festered underneath,
was Laelius offended, or Scipio,
who made a name for himself at Carthage?
Were they annoyed that Metellus got stung

and Lupus avalanched by apt satires?
Lucilius lampooned alike leaders
and common folk, tribe by tribe, favoring
only virtue and virtue's few friends.
Indeed, when valiant Scipio and wise,
kindly Laelius withdrew from public
matters, they took Lucilius along
and all three chortled while the cabbage boiled.
Lagging after Lucilius in rank
and wit, as I do, I've nonetheless lived
with the powerful, as Envy won't forget.
She'll hope to sink her fangs in something
soft when she strikes me, but she'll blunt them on
solid stuff. Learned Trebatius,
perhaps you disagree? *Trebatius:* Not at all.
But be careful and don't forget the law:
a man who writes scurrilous verse about
another can be called to account in court.
Horace: Scurrilous verse? Sure. But suppose
they're true, and good, and Caesar approves them?
Suppose the honest man who wrote such poems
pleads truth as his defense against libel?
Trebatius: The charge will get tossed out of court
with a snicker, and you'll laugh your way home.

SATIRE II, iv

Horace: Catius, where are you rushing
and from what? *Catius:* Home to jot down
some notes on the wisdoms I just heard.
Pythagoras, Socrates, and Plato—
they've been surpassed! *Horace:* Forgive me if I've
stopped you at a bad time, but that famous
memory of yours—a work of nature
or of art?—will track down all stray details.
Catius: It won't be easy. It's subtle stuff
and woven by a subtle mind. *Horace:* Who
is this wonder? A Roman? A stranger?
Catius: I can't tell you the maestro's name
but I already know his rules by heart.
The more oblong the egg and the less round,
the tastier, whiter and firmer; such
eggs have a male yolk. Cabbages grown on dry
land taste sweeter than the mushy pap raised
nearer to the city; all that water
spoils them. What if a friend drops in on you
at dinner time and the only chicken
you can catch is old, sinewy and tough?
To make it tender, dilute Falernian
with water and drown it in this birdbath.
Don't trust mushrooms not found in the meadows.
For good health all summer, top off your lunch
with black mulberries picked before the sun
is high. Aufidius mixed his honey
with strong Falernian—a disaster!

When the veins are empty, give them nothing
but bland tastes. A mild mead is just the thing
for sluicing out the stomach. If your bowels
get clogged, mussels will blaze a trail,
or any shellfish, or low-growing sorrel
(but only if combined with Coan wine).
Shellfish grow plumper as the new moon swells,
but you've got to know where the best of them
come from. The Lucine mussel is better
than the Baian cockle. The best oysters?
From Circeo. The choicest sea urchins?
From Cape Miseno. Luxurious
Tarentum is proud of its huge scallops.
You can't excel in the art of dining
unless you learn the theory of flavors.
It won't do just to buy inexpensive fish
unless you know which are better with sauce
and which fish, when broiled, will perk a tiring
diner up. The host who wants not to serve
dull meat will seek out an Umbrian boar
fattened on acorns from the holm-oak. Now
there's a porker that will bend the platter,
unlike the insipid Laurentian
boar that forages on marsh grass and reeds.
Deer who've grazed in the vineyards are not always
edible. The forelegs of a pregnant
rabbit please the gourmet most. As to fish
and fowl, my palate is the first to judge

exactly their prime age and quality.
Some specialize in finding new sweets,
but everything needs your attention.
Would you have your wines be excellent but
anoint your fish with an improper oil?
Set Massic wine out on a cloudless night—
its coarseness will be soothed, its nerve-jangling
bouquet will dissipate. But you can spoil
the same wine by straining it through linen,
sapping its strength. As for Surrentine wine,
an adept mixes it with the dark lees
of Falernian, then breaks a pigeon's egg
into the mixture. The slowly-sinking
yolk clasps all sediment in its grasp.
You can revive a burning drinker
with fried prawns or fried African snails.
No lettuce. It bobs on the stomach's acids
like a cork. Instead try ham and sausage,
or some hot tidbit from a street vendor.
Learn well the recipe for compound sauce.
The base is sweet olive oil. Mix it with
thick wine and brine in which fine Byzantine
fish have been packed. Mix with chopped herbs and boil.
Sprinkle with Corycian saffron, let
stand, then add some juice squeezed oh so gently
from the very best Vanafran olives.
Apples from Tibur look tastier than
those from Picenum, but they're not. Put up
Venuculan grapes, but smoke Alban grapes
until they're raisins. These last I was first
to serve with apples, as I was to serve

caviar in wine lees, or to sift black salt
and white pepper each mounded on its plate.
It's a crime to spend a small fortune
at the fish market and cramp the finny
giants on a narrow platter. Suppose
a slave has dandled the drinking cup
with hands greasy from filched snacks, or there's mold
on your best antique bowl? Wouldn't that turn
your stomach? Brooms, dishcloths, sawdust—how much
does it cost to fend off scandal? Would you
sweep mosaic pavements with a dirty
broom of palm-leaves, or toss grimy covers
on good upholstery? The less it costs to do
things right, the more's the blame if they're undone.
These are not cares only the rich can take.
Horace: Catius, you scholar, swear by the gods
and in the name of friendship that you'll take
me to the next lecture you attend.
Second-hand is second best; I want to see
this wizard for myself, as you have done.
I want to visit this pilgrim's fountain
and drink the precepts for a happy life.

ROGER MITCHELL
Lemon Peeled the Moment Before: New & Selected Poems (2008)

Roger Mitchell has received many honors for his work, including the Midland Poetry Award, the Akron Prize in Poetry, and two NEA Fellowships. For many years he taught in and directed the MFA program at Indiana University–Bloomington and was for ten years Director of that university's summer writers' conference. Today he lives in the Adirondack Mountains with his wife, the fiction writer Dorian Gossy.

In his own words: "I write poetry to find out what I know. The reasoning part of my mind knows some things, but not all. Not that much, in fact. It isn't too far-fetched to think of art–not just poetry–as a way of discovering the world and of fashioning one's place in it. That such basic concerns are also the basic concerns of philosophy, history, science, and religion comes as no surprise to me. Poetry is our ancient connection to a time when the boundaries between poet, philosopher, theologian, and scientist were porous. Poetry allows one, as Emerson exhorted us, to make 'an original relation to the universe,' not just one that's been handed down over the centuries. At the same time, poetry is an art—like all arts—with traditions, principally those of form and verbal acts like praise, lament, curse, and so forth. The challenge in writing it comes in choosing how closely to follow those traditions and how far to depart from them. Most poets can be found somewhere in the vast middle ground between rigid convention and pure (or attempts at pure) originality. There may be nothing new under the sun, as Solomon said, but we can (should?), as Pound urged, quoting an ancient Chinese philosopher, 'make it [the ordinary thing] new.'"

AUNT EL

She was said to have never bathed.
And to have stacked the rooms
of her house with newspapers.
I don't even know whose aunt she was.
Maybe nobody's aunt. Aunt Blank.
Though the glee in mother's eyes,
as she hands me the keys to this
damp closet, tells me, of course, what else.

I see her rattling about with a wagon
or bag, draped in a straggling dress
and bonnet, asking at back doors, cringing
under the stares of housegirls and cooks.
She couldn't have done it alone,
on her subscription, presuming she had one.
Presuming, too, she could read.
Maybe she needed to fill a room
in a hurry, to admire her handiwork,
to say, this is my room full of words.
She would say this to no one, of course,
thinking that no one would ever know.
There she is in a robe, tattered. She holds
the lantern away from her body,
as though she were paper herself.

There were farms somewhere
in back of my family, a barn
in back of my grandparents' house.
The people who live there now know nothing

about us, don't see the spot of blood
on the driveway, the ambulance idling
at the side door, don't see Aunt El
or her baffled eyes, going her rounds
in a stinking skirt, talking to dogs,
scattering children like flies. Even
the chickens avoided her mournful cluck.

Nor do they see the mayor of Avalon,
or the priest who lived with his sister,
the unmarried schoolteacher, the man
who ran out on his wife, or the one
who stole. They don't see the man
who killed himself drinking or the woman,
his wife, he left with the children,
or the chauffered limousine with someone,
concealed, in back. And certainly
they don't see Bertha, dead on the floor
of her unheated house in Camden.

I come from somewhere I've never been,
or somewhere I've been but don't remember.
I need to know that I've been where I've been
and lived there and loved what there was to love.
If I could, I would choose this woman, this aunt
whom no one mentioned (and no one forgot),
to take me there. She teaches me how to knock
at a back door, how to ask the smallest question.

THE STORY OF THE WHITE CUP

for Helen

I am not sure why I want to tell it,
since the cup was not mine, and I was not there,
and it may not have been white, after all.
When I tell it, though, it is white, and the girl
to whom it has just been given, by her mother,
is eight. She is holding a white cup to her breast,
and her mother has just said good bye, though those
could not have been, exactly, the words. No one knows
what her father has said, but when I tell it,
he is either helping someone very old with a bag
or asking a guard for a cigarette. There is, of course,
no cigarette. The box cars stand with their doors
slid back. They are black inside, and the girl
who has just been given a cup and told to walk
in a straight line and to look like she wants
a drink of water, who cried in the truck
all the way to the station, who knew, at eight,
where she was going, is holding a cup to her breast
and walking away, going nowhere, for water.
She does not turn, but when she has found water,
which she does, in all versions of the story, everywhere,
she takes a small sip of it and swallows.

THE WORD FOR EVERYTHING

There is the word for you
and beside it the word *me*,
though neither of us knows which they are.
There is the word for the two of us together
or apart. Together
and apart.
There is the word for chair,
the word *clear*.

There is the word for this moment, too,
though no one can pronounce it.
It is not now,
though there is the word *now*,
and the word *slow*.
Between them is the word
one does not hear,
the word these words look for,

here by the clear chair,
deep in the slow now.

THE PLACE WE CAME ASHORE

The small colony of black noddies
tucked up into its cave. The way
every time we go there, little spurts
of clouddust or shoremist spatter us
and on each of the narrow ledges up under
the glowering volcanic cap birdlime streaks
downward in a floral exuberance.
The sea comes heaving in on time, every time,
and the birds flap out now and again just
over the top of it. Try as hard as we can
to prevent it, they disappear into the light,
shredding itself to pieces on the sea's back.
I don't know why when I think of it, I think
this is the place love found us, away
almost from our own nature, looking back
up into the land as though from another world.
As though this was the place we came ashore
all those thousands of years ago, looking
for what we would learn to call each other.

MUSIC I KNEW

It was in Katowice, I think, in Silesia,
where the Polish border officials
in their snug uniforms of olive brown
boarded the trains going south into Czechoslovakia.
We were swarmed over in minutes by gypsies
going home for Christmas, assuming
that gypsies have a home, and Christmas.
Each year at that time those from the mines
and factories of southern Poland
go south into Czechoslovakia, and on,
I was told, into Hungary where gypsies,
briefly, cease being themselves and settle down.

Across from me the woman with no teeth
and black shining eyes had seven skirts
which she lifted like a bundle of laundry,
a handful of curtains, in search of a passport,
when the smiling border official slammed
the glass door back and shouted in seven languages
at once, none of them gypsy, "Passports, please."
Mine lay on my lap, the blank page turned.
The little gypsy girl, who also had seven skirts,
each for a time in her life when she would cease
being the person she was and start
being someone else, dodged among them
with a plastic bag full of passports,
collecting and dispensing at random,
to all her brothers and sisters, to all

her mothers and fathers, one jump ahead
of the trim border officials whose duty
to protect the state from disorder is hard,
who keep their minds on their high, clear task
and stamp with a small spring-loaded stamp,
eventually, whatever is laid before them.

I think it was that night, later,
after the gypsies had risen at Prague
in a body and burrowed into the darkness,
steam swirling along the platforms,
in search of a train that would take them
back into Hungary. Though who would have room
in Hungary to house these hundreds, with their skirts
and their bags full of fresh kohlrabi,
which they cut with a wide-bladed knife
on the thick flat pad of their thumbs
and eat in the same closed compartment as you
offering you some, too, which you take
and say, thank you, I come from America,
I live in a house, the night is cold.

It was then, that night,
when the gypsies were gone, when the spunk
and the sharp smell of kohlrabi stayed on
with the long sinews of tribes and the songs,
which we have only learned to disguise,
as we crept toward Vienna and Rome,
that the family from somewhere in central Europe got on.
And all night, as we rattled south toward the border
or waited, murmuring, on unlit sidings,

were slammed out of something like sleep
by several smiling officials, as our passports
were looked at and stamped and looked at again,
I watched, in the dim light, under the lid of sleep,
the mother, the father, two daughters, a son,
drink something clear from each other's glances.

It was a hot, cramped compartment on a train
crossing central Europe twenty years ago.
It was a night full of slammed doors and songs
sung in the back of my throat, as I slept
or pretended to sleep, as I crept forward
toward Vienna and Rome, the rest of my life,
listening to a music I had never heard, but knew,
a song I would come to sing, already mine.

STEVE ORLEN

This Particular Eternity (2001)
The Elephant's Child: New & Selected Poems (2006)

Steve Orlen is the author of six collections of poetry, including *The Bridge of Sighs* and *Kisses*. He has received awards from the John Simon Guggenheim Memorial Foundation and the National Endowment for the Arts, as well as the George Dillon Memorial Award from *Poetry* magazine. He teaches at the University of Arizona.

In his own words: "I learned how to tell stories at the feet of my father and my uncles. They always smoked cigars and made fun of each other. The stories they told went every which way. It took a long time before they'd get to the point, so I learned to be a patient listener. Most of my poems come from experience, and every experience has a narrative. When I sit down to write, I tell my stories the way my uncles did, not chronologically, but following whatever paths occur to me at the time. In fact, this is the way the mind moves. So, my job as a poet is to find something else besides chronological time to organize the material. And if I'm lucky, while I'm organizing I'll find out what the poem wants to be 'about'—what the theme might be. I think this quirk of mine has helped me to sort of re-invent the narrative poem."

MONKEY MIND

When I was a child I had what is called an inner life.
For example, I looked at that girl over there
In the second aisle of seats and wondered what it was like
To have buck teeth pushing out your upper lip
And how it felt to have those little florets the breasts
Swelling her pajama top before she went to sleep.
Walking home, I asked her both questions
And instead of answering she told her mother
Who told the teacher who told my father.
After all these years, I can almost feel his hand
Rising in the room, the moment in the air of his decision,
Then coming down so hard it took my breath away,
And up again in that small arc
To smack his open palm against my butt.
I'm a slow learner
And still sometimes I'm sitting here wondering what my father
Is thinking, blind and frail and eighty-five,
Plunged down into his easy chair half the night
Listening to Bach cantatas. I know he knows
At every minute of every hour that he's going to die
Because he told my mother and my mother told me.
I didn't cry or cry out or say I'm sorry.
I lay across his lap and wondered what
He could be thinking to hit a kid like that.

THE PAINTER

Clouds, and between them, sunlight scattering shadows on the road,
Then, when the road curved sharply, flowers, wild flowers, yellow
      poppies
Startling and spotting an upland meadow, surprising me out of my
      thoughts.
We'd been traveling. I had a little job to do. Gail had made a reservation
And the motel lady said it was for one night only, they were booked,
But the next morning there was a vacancy and the lady said, shaking
      her finger
Like a stern schoolteacher, *Don't forget to move your car*
When you switch rooms! We have only so many parking spaces.
We changed rooms, moving our small belongings, setting up house,
And there we were on a day trip to a ghost town on the mountain
      road
And there was the meadow, and I pointed—*Gail, will you look at*
      those flowers!
She had that look that said she was visiting another place inside her
      head,
A better place, a counter-universe where a painter could arrange
And rearrange flowers into birds that flew, the mountains into
      buildings
On the streets of Paris where the light had been so beautiful, so
      baffling,
Fixing its shadows to the stones, losing the stones and gaining more
      light,
That it drove her even further in. *I'm a tourist of the interior* she told
      me then.

Paris. She had walked relentlessly and daily for months, stopping,
    gazing,
Dreaming. Lost beside the Seine beside the sleeping *clochards*,
Making sketches, rushing back to our apartment to paint, to arrange
And rearrange *because*, she said, *the real world is just too much for me.
I can't deal with it*, and she would come out only for a moment
Because I asked and I asked because I didn't want to be
The only sane person left walking on the Place de la Republique.
Now she looked out at the yellow poppies and said, *What
Are they doing there?* Then she said, *Uh-Oh! We forgot to move our car!*
And I said, *Gail, we're in the car!* And she started crying.

MEN ON THE SHORE, FISH IN THE SEA

Some of the fathers were wading
Waist-deep in the shallows by the sand bar,
Their goggles piercing the water's surface, as though trolling,
The boys my age hanging around among the men
Not knowing what was going on, and a ways up from the water
The mothers on blankets with their books and lotions.

One man dove his right arm into the water
And came up with a handful of water.
Another bent his whole body in and disappeared,
Then came up spouting water. Dangling from his hand,
A fish the length of his arm—the sleek,
Evolved shape, six fins, a wide slash of mouth
With long, narrow, sharp double-rows of teeth
Dripping and glistening in the cave of its mouth.

The man stuck his fingers into the gill slits
And lifted it high in the air. *Sand shark,*
Someone said. *Mmm,* they said. *Mmm.*
The hand-catcher wheeled the shark
In a circle on the surface as if it were a toy fish
In a boy's bathtub. *Sharks swim,*
He said. *What does a sand-shark eat?*

A man grabbed a handful from the bottom
And stuffed it into the shark's mouth past the teeth.
Another. Another. Every time I go to a beach
I think about it. Though the mind may bristle at first,
There's always someone, then always someone else.

Some women strolled down to the water to cool off.
Unless you're going to eat it, let it go.

The hand-catcher looked around at the others, smiled
The smile sharks are born with and people learn
As one of many expressions available,
And the muscles of the face remember it.
The boys were seeing what it meant
To be a man among men and a man among women,

And who knows if any lasting decisions set in,
Either before the man flung the shark
Out past the sand bar to the deeps,
Or after, when whatever became of it
Was whatever was supposed to become of it.
Men on the shore. Fish in the sea.

A STAIRWELL, OUTSIDE A BANK

Through the iron bars, a stairwell, and in it
The shadows of the iron bars, black, aslant, severe,
And gray concrete steps going up and going down,
And a dark well of coolness rising like an echo,
But no one, nothing flourishing, astonishing or dying,
Until I finally asked myself what kept me there in reverie
Maybe five minutes before I went into the bank.
The other night I was strolling on Fourth Avenue,
The old sixties street where the retro-hippies
Lounge and beg, and the drunks
Walk with the crazies who carry Bibles
From The Second Free Will Baptist Church.
Strung among them, teenagers
Punked-out like metal flowers on display
Who watch with contempt the middle-aged
Entering the restaurants and looking back
With fear, or pity, or memories of the good old days
When questions still outnumbered answers.
The man who blocked my path
Seemed neither dangerous nor nuts.
About my height and age. A back-pack
And his boots looked sensible for miles of walking.
Are you a spiritual man? he asked.
And instead of answering glibly
I stood there and wondered what *spiritual* meant.
What people mean by it. I didn't engage the man.
What came to mind were iron bars and shadows, and the stairs, and
    no

Meaning in that but some beauty I must have seen,
Cold, as some beauty is, and momentary,
And through the gap between the beauty and the void
Something like an echo of water running over rocks.
If I felt lighter than my body
I didn't have the means to weigh it then.

      —for Tony Hoagland

THREE TEENAGE GIRLS: 1956

Three teenage girls in tight red sleeveless blouses and black Capri
        pants
And colorful headscarves secured in a knot to their chins
Are walking down the hill, chatting, laughing,
Cupping their cigarettes against the light rain,
The closest to the road with her left thumb stuck out
Not looking at the cars going past.

Every Friday night to the dance, and wet or dry
They get where they're going, walk two miles or get a ride,
And now the two-door 1950 Dodge, dark green
Darkening as evening falls, stops, they nudge
Each other, peer in, shrug, two scramble into the back seat,
And the third, the boldest, famous
For twice running away from home, slides in front with the man
Who reaches across her body and pulls the door shut.

THE ADVANTAGES OF
THE BARBARIANS

I had been reading History and gotten lost, so took my glasses off
And saw, not the eras described, their lists of terrible events,
But the moments shrunken and passed over, in footnotes with their
    asides
That tease the imagination. Not the great rivers,
But the drowned dragged out of a river into my little room,
Where they mill around and complain. Not the ancient map,
But that dip between mountains so narrow the cartographers over-
    looked it
On their lunch break, and there they are, that one man and that one
    woman,
Overlooked by History because when they hoe a rocky field they're
    so tiny,
And when they sleep in their straw mats they forget who they are.

ERIC PANKEY
Oracle Figures (2003), *Reliquaries* (2005)
The Pear As One Example: New & Selected Poems (2008)

Born in Kansas City, Missouri in 1959, **Eric Pankey** directed the MFA program at Washington University in St. Louis for many years. For the last decade he has taught in the MFA program at George Mason University where he is Professor of English and the Heritage Chair in Writing. He lives in Fairfax, Virginia, with his wife and daughter.

In his own words: "The poem is not a vessel for thought, a receptacle for what the poet has previously known. The poem is a way of thinking, a vehicle for that thinking, a way of writing toward what one does not know. Such a habit perhaps leads toward 'subjects' the certainty of which is always just beyond one's grasp and easy articulation."

THE RECONSTRUCTION
OF THE FICTIVE SPACE

I open my eyes and a season passes:
A single moth wing shudders on the sill.
The gate cannot open into the overgrown grass.

But the way, lit by foxfire and firefly,
By the flint-flash of grit at the pearl's heart,
Is a past words cannot return to history,

To what the swallows inscribe on the air,
And here, on the outskirts of memory,
I look off again into that distance,

As if into a future, the lightning opening
Before my eyes like Scripture.
The equation at hand can be proven

By the spiral descent of the fishhawk,
By the curve of a tiger-lily's stalk.
Yet all I see is surface glare,

An afterlife of the afterimage.

EPITAPH

Beyond the traceries of the auroras,
The fires of tattered sea foam,
The ghost-terrain of submerged icebergs;
Beyond a cinder dome's black sands;
Beyond peninsula and archipelago,
Archipelago and far-flung islands,
You have made of exile a homeland,
Voyager, and of that chosen depth, a repose.

The eel shimmers and the dogfish darts,
A dance of crisscrosses and trespasses
Through distillate glints and nacreous silts,
And the sun, like fronds of royal palm
Wind-torn, tossed, lashes upon the wake,
But no lamplight mars or bleaches your realm,
A dark of sediment, spawn, slough, and lees,
Runoff, pitch-black, from the rivers of Psalms.

HISTORY

A hundred flint arrowheads, chipped, rain-washed, scattered
  through a meadow of ragweed and clover,
The flesh they ripped, the rib nicked, the shields of horsehide torn,
  all lost to the elements;
An ice-pierced daybreak through a mica screen and the first lute
  arrives in China from Persia;

The uses of ambergris are perfected; the lamb's blood dries above
  the doorway; a glacier calves an iceberg;
From the rock where a father offered up his son as sacrifice, the
  Prophet ascends into paradise;
The summer you step on a rusted nail, the willows green and bend
  to the river; the river floods;

Before nightfall, a body is bargained for, secreted away in a borrowed
  grave fashioned from a cave;
Again, walls and towers topple. And no language but grief is left in
  common. And grief no language at all.
There is no history, only fits and starts, laughter at the table, lovers
  asleep, slaughter, the forgetfulness.

And yet for three nights straight, nothing but starlight—Byzantine,
  quicksilver, an emanation of a past—
And tonight you have renamed the constellations after the mudras:
  The Gesture Beyond Mercy,
*The Gesture for Warding Off Evil, The Gesture of Fearlessness, The Gift-
Bestowing Gesture of Compassion.*

THE MANDALA AND THE SQUARE

If all phenomena are empty, why does the underdrawing bleed
　　through:
A grid of hand-drawn horizontals, lines thinning to where the brush
　　is re-dipped,
The verticals snapped lines, the ink thickest at the point of impact;
　　the interstices
And hollows patched with indigo's luster, vermillion from cinnabar,
　　the red of lac,
Azurite, malachite, and other cuprous minerals on this orderly
　　model of the universe?

　　*

I cannot dispel the obstacles. Cannot hear the twilight language
　　beyond words. Try as I might.
I cannot step outside this well-fed furnace I call a body. Cannot
　　account for the hours.
Cannot reconstruct the sequence of events that was the day before
　　yesterday.
Cannot confirm my alibi. The long convalescence draws to a close.
　　I browse among the ruins.
As I look down, a garter snake slips between the gnarled roots of a
　　stump spiked with new growth.

"When I cover the square surface with rectangles, it lightens the
     weight of the square, destroys its power,"
Agnes Martin writes, regarding the hand-drawn grids afloat on her
     six by six canvases.
Yet in the very act of undermining the ideal she reiterates the
     revelations of its perfection.
How does one give in without giving up when one has mastered
     the conventions of closure?
"The way of the artist," she says, "is an entirely different way. It is a
     way of surrender."

          *

I broke a stick of rosemary wood and the resinous aroma—a hint
     of pine bark,
Even lavender, but more mineral than leaf or bloom—rose and I
     breathed it in.
The fragrance did not conjure memory, but had about it the essence
     of the *remembered*.
I sat on the front stoop killing time, almost happy in the warmth
     of mid-March sun,
Desiring this moment and not the next. Welcoming the next without
     desire.

THE NARRATION OF RAIN

Rain blows through the pines. Rain rattles water oak leaves. Rain on
      the stone chime.
Rain quick in rivulets and gullies. Rain on the river's broad back.
      Rain amid rain.
Rain fretting the rusty clay. Rain at a slant. Rain every which way
      but down.
Rain overflows the gutters. Rain marbles the picture window. Rain
      slips, stumbles, sluices.
Rain in the corn crib. Rain in the trough. Rain blows through the pines.

     *

The crow carries a bauble in its beak—something dully reflective—
And drops it onto the path of leaf mulch ahead, caws once, and
      lumbers up and low
Over the gauze of gnats, where wild blackberry overruns the
      unused train tracks.
I will leave the trinket for another to find.
                            I sidestep the omen.
      Ignore the oracle.
Having learned nothing from Sophocles as I put one foot in front
      of the other.

"Assyrians," the husband said, "are the first to use images to narrate."
(I eavesdrop in museums, a bad habit, I know, but one I prefer not
to set aside.)
The wife—I have assumed they are married, long married—nods *yes*.
"In archaic art," he says, "human faces are a blank.

                                                    Emotion is given
            to the hunted animals."
She furrows her brow and nods *yes*. Dubious. Holding back some
rebuttal.

        *

I have never heard the nightingale nor beheld the manzanita;
I know nothing of the gods: their tedium, their melancholy, their
        blood's leaden sludge.
But I have made a narration of rain as it blows through the pines,
        as it slips, stumbles, and sluices;
The rain as a scattered body; the rain as shape-shifter; the rain as
        blessing;
The rain on the face of the hunter and on the sorrowful face of the
        prey.

PASTORAL INTERIOR

I keep to myself. I keep quiet.
I keep quiet. I keep to myself.

The water in the glass is darker than the glass.
The water is heirloom silver left to tarnish.

I keep calibrating the gravity of minutia.
I keep a secret as if it were an antidote.
I keep time by the slow work of rust,

By words cut loose from their moorings:
Cove, clove, cleave . . .

I am listening to "May Sheep Safely Graze,"
As the water in the glass grows darker than the glass.

The twilight—vestigial, lupine—lingers.

RESTLESS GHOST

The wasps' paper nest hung all winter.
Sun, angled in low and oblique,
Backlit—with cold fever—the dull lantern.

Emptied, the dangled nest drew him:
Gray. Translucent. At times an heirloom
Of glare, paper white as burning ash.

Neither destination nor charm, the nest
Possessed a gravity, lured him, nonetheless,
And he returned to behold the useless globe

Eclipse, wane and wax. He returned,
A restless ghost in a house the wind owns,
And the wind went right through him.

KATHLEEN PEIRCE
The Ardors (2004)

Kathleen Peirce is the author of three previous collections: *Mercy* (U. of Pittsburgh Press), which won the Associated Writing Programs Prize, *Divided Touch, Divided Color* (Windhover Press), and *The Oval Hour* (University of Iowa Press), which won the Iowa Prize and the William Carlos Williams Award from the Poetry Society of America. She teaches at Texas State University.

In her own words: "The demand is to stay in the physical world as deeply as possible while opening the interior world farther than expected, and trusting language to be the most wild and most loyal companion. If the mind is wider than the sky, (and it is), the line can be (like a mind) larger than the space that contains it. I love that the making of lines signals edges both made and found, and that for all their possibilities in form, they move forward by breaking."

FROM UNDERNEATH

When we were untouched by human voices,
we could hear music played, and we were not unlike
the selves we brought to animals
whose presences were instruments of love
almost without fail. We saw birds every day;
before we slept we often thought of how those fly
who fly at night, not the dark topfeathers
serrating another dark, but the pale
underfeathers hidden by a wing that could, and had
glanced back. Fish also kept a paleness underneath;
don't think we weren't afraid. Our stillness
was pearl-stillness; if we were radiant
it was a radiance accrued while having been contained.
We wondered why to shell is to pry out. Music was beautiful,
fathomless in a way we understood, the notes most often
falling at the end like words in sentences, pearls in water,
animals, blue sky. We understood that in the time it took
each chord to play, some of us would die. Some continued
being held; others were holding still and listening.

BLACK PEARL

The arm is lowered, the wrist is flexed
as to present the palm more or less
parallel to the ground—not unlike
a natural gesture of supressing. This way
we showed we loved, not the dead,
but ourselves remembering what those
once living thought about,
those now dissolved by what-nots making up the dirt,
blurred and engulfed maybe the same as any object
approached in increments by light, and we were changed
softly as when we thought about the stars
when the sky was blue. There were lilies
named star-gazer; their buds were fits of color
pushing into light, but their scent, it seemed,
was another way to think of radiance, like thoughts
we thought the dead once had, the dead
the earth and heaven had made far from us.

THE ROOMS

When we dreamed of rooms
we knew that entering can cause a place to be,
as when a pearl is a worm's dream,
accrued by a layering of substances outside itself
of which it is the cause. So it was with our
dream-rooms, which we always felt we had
discovered more than made.
In our dream-rooms, our mothers were young again,
while the fur on the magnolia pods remained the same
as in our wakeful lives, and water did, wearing water's face.
Hallways, doorways. We were helpless going in,
unable to die there, and when we woke
we knew we had been shaped, not loved
as pearls are loved; we were not removed.

HALL OF LIGHT

In the way the orange canary's phrase protruded
in the quiet of the room, there was the passing of
a sunflower seed across a gap between two cardinals
outside, and the final color of the grass achieved
the rosiest of its browns. In the way a solitary thought
keeps hid a chamber, lit only by reflections
on its inner walls of jade and gold, we could feel
absence as a bird's indifference to the color
of a leaf, being the most lucid thing among a field of leaves,
or a hawk's indifference to the passage of a labial cloud
above its back, or a breast-cloud, or a mouth. Do you hear
how morning feels? There is singing where you are?

PEARL

Sometimes we wanted to last longer
with our eyes closed, to know a day
as each of us had known interiors
of each mother once,
or to exaggerate our dream lives
into shared experience, or to see
if darkness projected on an object
altered it, as we seemed altered every night.
So we were pearls, or tried to feel ourselves
to be the thoughts of pearls. It was difficult
being still among the most still things,
but where we found bodies of trees attached
to earth, we were reassured, except their leaves
were like our dreams, unapproachable as a mass,
and each carrying the tense fragility of skin.
Then things stopped resembling us
the more we touched or thought of them.
By the time we could be carried into water,
formless, viscous, scented with the deaths,
we were most afraid, and most aware that to be held
is different than to be healed, but not by much.
Which led us to behold, and our eyes looked,
and some could see beloveds everywhere.

THE BELLS BREAK DOWN
THEIR TOWER

If we hadn't been lonely, could we have sensed,
both underwater and in air, the tendencies
of flickering? So many moved that way:
fish, wing, hand, star, branch at sunrise,
branch in water, branch on fire.
We were constant, or felt that our will was,
even as we pulsed and blinked, and it was
our constancy that made us want to enter
smaller things with confidence,
and larger things with fear. So it was easier
to feel more longing for our equals than our gods.
A single snail baffled us. Had it made its shell with its secretions
or had it found itself? And then of course the snail
crept away. But the pearls we strung were lunar, luminous,
tellurian, and still. Draped across a woman's breast,
they tempered us, who were constantly drawn to sites of sustenance
without the memory of having eaten there, where gradually
we found ourselves most often trembling and wavering and loose.

QUIET LINES

We wanted to be seen by our mothers
but our mothers were falling down,
and though we tried to think of falling
as the inversion of ascent, our thinking failed
for we had not ascended very far,
even by middle age, or if we had,
we had been taught to feel our heights discreetly,
as titmice might feel while waiting in a cypress
for the rain to stop, and wasn't fall
beautiful, the cypress leaves more feather-like in brown.
When our mothers entered the familiar rooms
and looked at us, and knew not who we were,
we were not anonymous, we were more shell than pearl
is all, opened to the limit at the hinge: wings for a doll to wear.
No pearl; pearls roll away. So we remember them.

IMAGINARY LINES

When we said logic was transcendental,
we felt other words we might have said
find form the way shadows find form, with dependence
on things both intimately close and infinitely separate,
palpable as the sky palpating with a blue we saw
and loved and never felt surrounded by,
palpable as what we saw with our eyes closed.
We could feel the unsaid begin to touch our mouths
the same way shadows began first where two things met
and might be parted, where touch obscured
a body's edge so brilliantly.
How casually the light declined. The roundest pearls
gave way to oval shadows. Mornings we found
it snowed all night. There was often a feeling of rest gathering
to meet itself outside ourselves; there was the feeling
that thinking one thing had caused another thing to be.

WHITE SHELLS

Then there was beauty in what clung,
vertical and multiple against a damp tombstone
where no one goes, or has gone forever,
the stone carved in another language
and the weed-life overgrown.
We knew they must know movement,
but they would not move
while being what they meant to us.
Where the headstone's windowpane,
meant to protect the crucifix and photograph,
was cracked apart, we saw how
on its inward, wetter side,
the infant shells began self-generation in a line
like vowels strung inside a child's understanding:
this belongs to this. O perfect succulence
with which interiors adhere to forms, O open mouths.
Should we have found the world more often
clinging to words describing it?
What would have been the afterlife of that?

JOSH RATHKAMP
Some Nights No Cars at All (2007)

Josh Rathkamp's work has appeared in numerous literary journals, including *Indiana Review, Meridian, Passages North, Puerto Del Sol, Gulf Coast, Sycamore Review, Verse Daily,* and *The Drunken Boat.* Rathkamp has received awards from the Arizona Commission for the Arts, has been named the Arizona representative for the National Arts and Letters Society and a Virginia G. Piper writing fellow. He is currently the Coordinator of Creative Writing at Mesa Community College. *Some Nights No Cars At All* is his first book of poetry.

In his own words: "Much of the work in my first book has its other possibilities—by which I mean a wholly new and startling landscape that is the acolyte deserts of Arizona. Living here on the moon, as it were, and for half of the year in nearly unbearable temperatures, something altogether interior visited me. The experience of this landscape is confused by its actual history—on the one hand, geological, on the other hand, recent and territorial, and in the great middle ranges, the profound consciousness of Anasazi and Hohokam. They say, here, just to walk on the ground is to dream. And I think my book is about dreams—how sometimes before bed my daughter asks me to drag my fingers softly across her back—to help, to find peace in sleep."

SPECTATORS ALONG
THE INTERSTATE

A few miles outside Kalamazoo we wonder
how on earth the first spring storm

blew the roof off a barn,
sent it dragging-ass like a barge out to sea.

On the news a farmer stood sure
of its connection to God; *it's representational*, he said,

as if the roof had perched on a church steeple.
By morning its picture plastered everywhere

brought people believing in miracles,
the roof in all its ridiculousness,

still erect, flown over the highway
in a perfectly flocked V. It's not hard to imagine

the spectators along the interstate,
the wet stuck smell of a wet corn field,

the roof, a big roof so sick of the years
of its body it had to let go, say yes to the wind,

yes to the water, yes to the earth that knows
the powerful and the beautiful have different names.

LOSING

Behind the iron trellis is where I found him,
searching the burnt brown ground

for a small sparkle, the hint of something shining steel.
His wife was going to kill him,

he said, in a manner which meant his meaning
was more serious than true. He only threw the ball

and before he knew his wedding ring flew from his finger
in a direction even God, he was sure, was unsure about.

The porch light lit small
stretches of the yard; it lit low limbs of the citrus;

it lit John, there beneath it, parting
the blades of grass with his hands until his hands

became lost, incapable of doing anything,
even separating.

I JUST CALLED TO SAY

Each night I'd dream she'd wait a while in silence,
letting the words of the song or the sound of my voice
carry a current that swept over the roof top,
through the empty arms of the sycamore.
She lived two blocks away, and, in eighth grade,
I thought Stevie Wonder had as good a shot as any
at getting me laid. All I had to do was pick up the phone
and sing a song about picking up a phone.
I'd play the way the song would sound in my head.
I'd be singing, nailing notes, imagining the girl
I loved loving every minute of it.
She'd wait there, as I said, in silence, twirling
stray strands of her hair around her finger,
motioning with her free hand to her friends,
for them to come over and listen.
I thought that this was the way to win
her heart. For once, I could be somebody
who knew how to woo a girl
into love and sex, so it could come, and come,
to me, naturally. When I told my brother my plan
he called me a pussy and said I sang like shit.
Still, I thought, somehow, someway, I could be the one
so many boys talked about:
tougher than Tommy's fifth grade quiz
when he herded us into the last stall of the boys' bathroom
and showed us a picture of a bent
over bare woman's ass, and asked, which hole
was which. And although I knew I'd never be Tommy,

that when I answered him wrong
it would follow me for life, although I knew
my friends would taunt me, I thought
that this song and the way I could sing it
could make a girl make me a man.
But now, it seems, no one laughs
at the way we want love. Just last week
when I returned the last stack of my ex's cds,
no one laughed when
it took three turns around the block to pull in.

THE MESSENGER

for John Espinoza

I think the bird that shit on your shoulder is not a messenger of God
as you said, but only a bird, a bird that chose the tree above us.
But, also as you said, what if the bird was racist?
It could have landed on that branch spotting a darker man.
I'd have to think the opposite though.
I'd have to think that sometimes birds hide too
behind laughter. They must want. They must need to ride
a bike or drive 65 in a car without wind
smearing tears to their faces. The question is then
was it bliss or hate that the bird felt for you.
Was it a joke, the way we are all jokes to someone else as they talk
sweetly in bed? What difference John,
the way we get shit on ourselves?
It is bound to happen. We are bound to the earth
just as birds are bound to sky.
Sometimes what we think is soaring is actually
a hell of a lot of work.

WHAT'S WRONG
WITH BEING HUMAN

I lived two houses down a dead end street.
When the river ran rough
we checked our basements.
We called to each other to help.
We hauled boxes up
from the dark like large fish.

When Mary or Mark or Helen died,
little by little,
we all did. We sent flowers.
The street took to looking
like a Cadillac. It grew bolder.
It grew rosy cheeks.

When Jack repainted, John
repainted, and the painters
ate lunch on the roof.

We said *it looks nice*,
nodding at our mailboxes.
We waved while shoveling snow
off the walkway no one walked
but the dogs and our manic-depressive mailman.

When we wanted an egg or a glass
of milk we drove to the store.
We stared out our windows.
Our children grew without parents.
We grew into speaking without words.

We thought our reflections
in the lamplight were only there
out of loyalty, and, if given
a chance, would run
like Mrs. Eddie's dead son
naked, through trees.

JUNE IN THE DESERT

Tonight relentless fires burn
an hour north of here.
At work we set out reamed boxes
of old paper to collect money
because there are so many
needy and how
can things be all right.

Last night my girlfriend said
that there wasn't a burning
between us, nothing that would make
het tape her life to mine,
but still we decide to wait
for something to grow
into something else.

How selfish it is to think
this way about fire,
about wanting it, about wishing
it could spread through the pines
with so much devastation
when it comes, it comes
big enough to burn us down.

TATTOO

When I turned sixteen and found my license
read '74 not '79, Peanut drove for the twelve pack
we drank too quickly at the drainage creek,
throwing our empties at the robins in the trees,
which would take off, in panic, and return,
take off and then return.

It was a game the birds knew. Soon we would leave,
soon the rotting apple of the sky would darken.
And when it did, we did.
We walked two blocks to the tattoo shop.
We flipped pages of anchors,
of anchors and waves, of big anchors splashing

like a whale's tail before a face appeared, a demon with a tongue
that curled. I thought I was living. A car, no curfew,
no black eye, and a buzz.
I wanted to be crazy, not end up like my father
or brothers or friends who have grown roots
too long in a town surrounded

by streams. Now, we're no different, them
and me. Our imperfections. There is a fiery face
on my leg I see before bed, a face on my leg
not mine. And I remember my father
placing his soft hand over it, pleading
how's it come off, how's it come off?

JAMES RICHARDSON
Vectors: Aphorisms & Ten-Second Essays (2001)
Interglacial: New & Selected Poems (2004)

James Richardson's *Interglacial: New and Selected Poems and Aphorisms* was a finalist for the National Book Critics Circle Award. His previous books include *Vectors: Aphorisms and Ten-Second Essays*, and *How Things Are* (2000), as well as two critical studies. Recipient of an Award in Literature from the American Academy of Arts and Letters, the Robert H. Winner, Cecil Hemley and Emily Dickinson Awards of the Poetry Society of America, and fellowships from the NEH and the New Jersey State Council on the Arts. His favorite reading, aside from poetry, is science and science fiction. He is Professor of English and Creative Writing at Princeton University.

In his own words: "It is with poetry as with love: forcing yourself is useless, you have to want to. Yet how tiresome and ungenerous is the one sprawled among flowers all day waiting for his impulse. There's such a thing as knowing how to make yourself want to.

Reading is living faster than life, writing is living slower.

The audience is faceless, back rows disappearing into dimness, and it doesn't talk back. Find your audience and you will blather. Write, instead, to a listener at your table for two, the one in your head whose faint blush, half-smile, glazed eyes make you correct course in mid-sentence, back off, explain, stop to listen.

Why would we write if we'd already heard what we wanted to hear?

Sure, no one's listening, English will die in a hundred years, and the far future is stones and rays. But here's the thing, you Others, you Years to Come: you do not exist.

There, all along, was what you wanted to say. But this is not what you wanted, is it, to have said it?"

from VECTORS: APHORISMS AND TEN-SECOND ESSAYS

1. The road reaches every place, the short cut only one.

2. Those who demand consideration for their sacrifices were making investments, not sacrifices.

3. What you give to a thief is stolen.

4. Despair says *I cannot lift that weight.* Happiness says, *I do not have to.*

5. You've never said anything as stupid as what people thought you said.

6. Our avocations bring us the purest joys. Praise my salads or my softball, and I am deified for a day. But tell me I am a great teacher or a great writer and you force me to tell myself the truth.

7. Ah, what can fill the heart? But then, what *can't?*

8. Shadows are harshest when there is only one lamp.

9. Desire's most seductive promise is not pleasure but change, not that you might possess your object but that you might become the one who belongs with it.

10. I say nothing works any more, but I get up and it's tomorrow.

11. A beginning ends what an end begins.

12. I walk up the drive for the morning paper and find myself musing, as if the news were fiction, *Marvelous that they think of all this, so deadpan strange*. Nothing is so improbable as the truth. If the day's headlines hadn't already happened, they would not happen.

13. Gravity's reciprocal: the planet rises to the sparrow's landing.

14. When a jet flies low overhead, every glass in the cupboard sings. Feelings are like that: choral, not single; mixed, never pure. The sentimentalist may want to deny the sadness or boredom in his happiness, or the freedom that lightens even the worst loss. The moralist will resist his faint complicity. The sophisticate, dreading to be found naive, will exclaim upon the traces of vanity or lust in any motive, as if they were the whole. Each is selling himself simplicity; each is weakened with his fear of weakness.

15. Road: what the man of two minds travels between them.

16. The cynic suffers the form of faith without its love. Incredulity is his piety.

17. Pessimists live in fear of their hope, optimists in fear of their fear.

18. Writer: how books read each other.

20. If the couple could see themselves twenty years later, they might not recognize their love, but they would recognize their argument.

21. Each lock makes two prisons.

22. Painting high on the house. Yellow jackets swarmed around me. I couldn't convince them I was harmless, so I had to kill them.

23. All stones are broken stones.

24. Of all the ways to avoid living, perfect discipline is the most admired.

26. It is by now proverbial that every proverb has its opposite. For every *Time is money* there is a *Stop and smell the roses*. When someone says *You never stand in the same river twice* someone else has already replied *There is nothing new under the sun*. In the mind's arithmetic, 1 plus -1 equals 2. Truths are not quantities but scripts: Become for a moment the mind in which this is true.

27. The viruses that co-opt the machinery of our cells; the stories we allow to enter and explain us.

28. If the wise knew everything the foolish know, there would be no fools.

29. Pain is not a democracy.

MY GODZILLA

Much of the monster movie was (bah DUMMM)
suspense. The coastal fog, the lo-rez video.
You couldn't see him, he was going to be worse than anything,
worse than your worst fears, namely . . .
how could they be your worst if you could know?
Forty years on: you're pretty sure what's coming.
He pokes from the distressingly fragile harbor,
black-tiled, sky-scraping penis, looking a little worse,
for having been nuked and long under water,
but not bad for a penis. *Who's going to clean it up?*
you think, that mess he's making. Also,
that it's fine, his stomping through the gridlock
with a distinctly rubbery wobble,
swatting the haze of planes, drop-kicking taxis.
So maybe he'll snack on the falsetto lovers?
The script, alas, is not what time re-writes.
He's how you look in your bathrobe in the morning,
how you keep smashing through the day,
fired at, invisibly hurt, intent,
litter of ages swirling around your ankles,
the *grit grit grit* of your soles, those tiny, unheard cries.

ALL THE GHOSTS

Their dream decelerates the spinning planet
one millimeter-per-second per century,
until, our slowness slowly matching theirs,
they can stride into our lives and live again—

a matter of eons, nothing to them, so patient,
since the massed wish of all the dead
is only the slide of a hem across a floor,
or the difference on your face of milder air.

It is their fate, they murmur. It is anyway their way
to shun the theatrical or gothic gesture.
They would not rattle chains if chains could hold them.
It is the wind, so much stronger, that slams doors.

They are heard, if ever, in the dramas of your dreams
where you cannot tell still voices from your own,
intervening, if at all, in the neural substrate,
shunting a lone electron *Maybe* or *Maybe not.*

Theirs are evasive and oblique persuasions,
stone by stream, for example, snows on outer planets,
undetected constants haunting physicists,
eddies where time runs sidelong or remembers.

Their delight is yielding, wind within the wind,
to faint velleities or fainter chances,
for they find among death's consolations, few enough,
the greatest is, to be mistaken for what happens.

When your eyes widen, they are surging to observe
the evening's trend to mauve, and all you have chosen
so slowly you are unaware of choosing.
And you may feel them feel, amused or touched

(history has not been long enough to decide which)
when your blunt patience emulates their own,
when you sense, like them, all fate might well be focused
in the exact glint of a right front hoof uplifted,

when you wait, as they must, for that crisis of precision
when it will make all the difference in the world
whether a particular petal's sideslipping fall
hushes the rim of a glass, or misses.

DEATH

He's not the Scyther, black hood, face in shadow;
still less the sinuous and cuff-linked Flourisher
of those cigarettes you can't buy anywhere;
and least of all the Seductress with a plan.
Since he dies repeatedly, Death has no experience.
When you meet, it might as well be his first time.
If there's a reason you should go, he's clueless.
If saintliness or subtlety of heart
in a universe just faintly just would save you,
he's much too young to understand,
but don't say that. Really he wasn't thinking
particularly of you, this teen with a too-big Uzi
he doesn't even know yet if he's going to use.

LATE SNOW

There's always a chance it won't like stopping,
will warm to the idea of going on and on
through April, to see for itself what's happening
beyond the yellow walls of daffodils,
and what May's like, that hour it has never stayed up till.
Will beg to be allowed to watch from a distance
the rumor of June, that afterland, July,
will be flexible to get what it wants, conceding
even on temperature and color
to snow warmly and invisibly
over your short-sleeved guests in August,
a slight dilution of their upheld wine.
It promises to be good, will moderate
its obsession with the hexagon
and tendency to drift, until at last
it can't be told from the stiffness of your rising,
a little late, in the latter days of summer,
from the dry clear downpour of the sun,
from your dream of the early snow still weeks and weeks in the future.

SEIDO RAY RONCI
The Skeleton of the Crow: New & Selected Poems (2008)

Seido Ray Ronci is a Zen monk and the director of Hokoku-An Zendo in Columbia, MO. He was a lay-student of Kyozan Joshu Sasaki-Roshi for twenty years before being formally ordained in 1999. The author of five chapbooks and a full-length collection (*This Rented Body*, Pressed Wafer, 2006), Ronci teaches in the English Department at the University of Missouri in Columbia.

In his own words: "This book contains over thirty years of work. Without intending it, I wrote a spiritual autobiography in poetry. I once was a young poet who practiced Zen; over the years I became a formally ordained Zen monk who practices poetry. This book follows that transition in terms of both content and form. The very early poems are the poems of a young man under the influence of poetry. But as the years pass, the influences shift. The poems become more sparse, less poetic, more direct. The Zen practice becomes more apparent. There is a kind of implicit narrative to the book that I never intended. It's the story of a man seeking a path and then finding one. That doesn't mean the journey is over, it just means that the path has been found and here we go!"

CROSSING THE WATER

Most of the years I have let the lights
and miles amaze me, let the lips and hair send
me over the oceans and back, let the legislators
of intelligence publish excuses for my repeated
seductions; for the graves in the war zone,
for the balcony and gazebo, the vine and venom.
I could not climb any mountains because
the smoke in my lungs and the glasses clinking,
the eyes on me; the dim, velvety
conversations kept me bound
to the leather wingback, the fire ablaze and young,
no reason to be other than young until
years pressed seed from blossom
and mother enjoyed fulfillment in flower
and flower to be.
This is how the glass reaches the lips
and the liquor courses. This, in every direction
goes as Holiness in sinner and holiness
as Savior. It is that which makes the gods
muscular with goodness, and the devils geniuses
of evil. It is that which maintains what comes
and must go, that change that keeps the world
the same people, the same gods and lack of gods,
the same fugitives and saints.
I am no thief. Nothing is, nor ever can be,
mine.

SNOW

On our way out the door, my three-year-old son says,
"Dad, I have to poop."
After all the work of bundling him up,
"Go ahead," I say.
He sheds his parka, drops his snow pants,
and mounts the high white seat of the toilet.
I unbutton my overcoat, loosen my scarf,
let it hang from my neck, and wait.
Almost immediately he calls from the bathroom,
"Papa, check my bottom."
I lean over the small of his back as he bows
lost in the flurry of my overcoat and scarf.
I wipe his ass again. He hops off the toilet,
pulls up his pants. I flush and see shit
on the fringe of my scarf; disbelieving,
I hold it up to the light:
"There's shit on my scarf!"
He puts on his coat, mittens and hat.
I'm reminded of the young monk Ikkyu
wiping Kaso's shriveled ass with his bare hands,
washing his master's frail body, rinsing
the soiled sheets, wringing them out
day and night till the old man's death.
I think, too, of the stains on my father's bed,
the nurses drawing the curtains to clean him,
his sunken eyes, looking into mine, ashamed.
"It's all right, Dad," I say.
"It's not all right," he says.

My son tromps to the door, flings it open:
a blast of cold air rushes through the house.
I wash the fringe in the sink, tighten
my scarf and raise my collar.
He's making angels in the snow.

BICYCLE

Locked to the fence, the chain links
overgrown with ivy, the handle bars,
seat, front fork, spokes, tires all
in a snare of green leaves and blue buds.
Tires soft, almost flat. Rust forming
where the frame's chipped and scarred.
Even the lock, caked with orange, seems
impossible to undo. Each day as I pass you
locked in the grip of the dense vines,
I miss the banking and turning, following
the wind one moment, fighting it the next,
keeping an eye on the clouds, planning
where to lock you in case of rain.
The breeze lifts the morning glories
from your blue metallic frame. Small
consolation, this retirement
among the sprawling, leafy vines
and abundant blossoms. You've become
a trellis: no longer a moving thing,
but a thing moved upon.

CRICKET

In the bush outside my window
you say the same thing over and over
with equal enthusiasm. Whatever it is,
I know it's the truth. No one could go on
so relentlessly if it wasn't.
What the truth is doesn't matter, finally,
because of your persistence.
I could hear you saying *cricket-cricket*
and translate it to *I am-I am!*
And just as easily I could hear the chirping
Fuck-it-fuck it! and be equally moved
because I'm here by the window
where the stars are, where the half moon is.
Each morning, turning off the alarm,
stepping from the shower, drying myself,
tying my shoes, packing my bag . . .
When a car comes you become silent.
Too much noise shuts us both up.
Like you, I disappear all day.

from THE SKELETON
OF THE CROW

The dead sing
under the grass.

Press your ear
to the tombstone

listen to the songs
you'll sing.

*

Stepping into heaven,
stepping into hell.

Big deal! *No one*
is the one

who walks away
from both.

*

Sometimes
I'm just a storm

pouring myself
onto everything—

then the mosquitos
rule the porch.

Gray-haired lust:
ignorance grass.

One beautiful woman
after another

doing her errands
enters my sleep.

*

All night, cicadas and crickets.

I brush my teeth
wash my face.

Put the skeleton down,
let the skeleton dream.

*

*Being and non-being
embrace and separate—*

without thinking
I swat the mosquito on my head.

Seeing, I wipe our blood
on my sleeve.

Is there a god or isn't there?
Is there a me or isn't there?

Answer one
you answer both.

In the meantime,
black tea while it rains.

*

These books on my shelf
like lovers I remember

who changed my life
for better, for worse.

*

My youth is gone, still
I raise the ax high

let it drop on its own
to split log after log

no matter how many times
I miss and groan

again.

The gates of heaven,
the gates of hell,

kick them open hard
and arrive exactly

where home sweet home
has always been.

*

Tonight the sun
a bright ripe plum

robbed me of
old age and memories—

come sunset
the same old me.

*

Once you visit no-man's-land
it's clear—

In the beginning was the word.

If that doesn't make you laugh,
nothing will.

CHARLES SIMIC
The Monster Loves His Labyrinth (Notebooks, 2008)

Charles Simic, U.S. Poet Laureate from 2007—2008, is the author of numerous books of poetry, including *The World Doesn't End*, which won the Pulitzer Prize. Simic was the 2007 recipient of the Wallace Stevens Award from the Academy of American Poets, in recognition of his "outstanding and proven mastery in the art of poetry." He is Emeritus Professor of the University of New Hampshire, where he has taught since 1973.

In his own words: "After a while it becomes an obsession, or an extension of obsession. You need it for your own daily existence. Then it becomes an intellectual obsession. Like any other art, you're thinking of your contemporaries, and your very strong feeling, especially when you're very young, is that your contemporaries don't know what the hell they're doing. So you have to straighten out the world. And eventually you also have all kinds of aesthetic theories. So it gets complicated. It becomes an ongoing complication, and the literary world, happily, is unfriendly. It's not like, when you're young, people are jumping up and down, saying, 'Oh, my God! Another poet! Aren't we lucky!' Essentially, it's, 'Get away, creep! Out of my sight!' And this all fuels a kind of passion and soul-searching and obsession. It's a true obsession. At that point, you can't help yourself. You just work." —from an interview with Ray González in *The Bloomsbury Review*.

Late night on MacDougal Street. An old fellow comes up to me and says: "Sir, I'm writing the book of my life and I need a dime to complete it." I give him a dollar.

Another night in Washington Square Park, a fat woman with fright wig says to me: "I'm Esther, the goddess of Love. If you don't give me a dollar, I'll put a curse on you." I give her a nickel.

One of those postwar memories: a baby carriage pushed by a hump-backed old woman, her son sitting in it, both legs amputated.

She was haggling with the greengrocer when the carriage got away from her. The street was steep so it rolled downhill with the cripple waving his crutch, his mother screaming for help, and everybody else laughing as if they were in the movies. Buster Keaton or somebody like that about to go over a cliff . . .

One laughed because one knew it would end well. One was surprised when it didn't.

I didn't tell you how I got lice wearing a German helmet. This used to be a famous story in our family. I remember those winter evenings just after the War with everybody huddled around the stove, talking and worrying late into the night. Sooner or later, it was inevitable, somebody would bring up my German helmet full of lice. They thought it was the funniest thing they ever heard. Old people had tears of laughter in their eyes. A kid dumb enough to walk around with a German helmet full of lice. They were crawling all over it. Any fool could see them!

I sat there saying nothing, pretending to be equally amused, nodding my head while thinking to myself, what a bunch of idiots! All of them! They had no idea how I got the helmet, and I wasn't about to tell them.

It was in those first days just after the liberation of Belgrade, I was up in the old cemetery with a few friends, kind of snooping around. Then, all of a sudden, we saw them! A couple of German soldiers, obviously dead, stretched out on the ground. We drew closer to take a better look. They had no weapons. Their boots were gone, but there was a helmet that had fallen to the side of one of them. I don't remember what the others got, but I went for the helmet. I tiptoed so as not to wake the dead man. I also kept my eyes averted. I never saw his face, even if sometimes I think I did. Everything else about that moment is still intensely clear to me.

That's the story of the helmet full of lice.

Beneath the swarm of high-flying planes we were eating watermelon. While we ate the bombs fell on Belgrade. We watched the smoke rise in the distance. We were hot in the garden and asked to take our shirts off. The watermelon made a ripe, cracking noise as my mother cut it with a big knife. We also heard what we thought was thunder, but when we looked up, the sky was cloudless and blue.

My mother heard a man plead for his life once. She remembers the stars, the dark shapes of trees along the road on which they were fleeing the Austrian army in a slow-moving ox-cart. "That man sounded terribly frightened out there in the woods," she says. The cart went on. No one said anything. Soon they could hear the river they were supposed to cross.

In my childhood women mended stockings in the evening. To have a "run" in one's stocking was catastrophic. Stockings were expensive, and so was electricity. We would all sit around the table with a single lamp, my grandmother reading the papers, we children pretending to do our homework, while watching my mother spreading her red-painted fingernails inside the transparent stocking.

In the biography of the Russian poet, Marina Tsvetaeva, I read that her first poetry reading in Paris took place on February 6, 1925, and the newspaper announcement says that there were also three musicians on the program, Madame Cunelli, who sang old Italian songs, Professor Mogilewski, who played violin, and V. E. Byutsov, who was on piano. This was astonishing! Madame Cunelli, whose first name was Nina, was a friend of my mother's. They both studied with the same voice teacher, Madame Kedrov, in Paris, and then somehow Nina Cunelli ended up in Belgrade during the Second World War where she taught me Russian and French children's songs, which I still know well. I remember that she was a beautiful woman, a little older than my mother, and that she went abroad after the War ended.

There was a maid in our house who let me put my hand under her skirt. I was five or six years old. I can still remember the dampness of her crotch and my surprise that there was all that hair there. I couldn't get enough of it. She would crawl under the table where I had my military fort and my toy soldiers. I don't remember what was said, if anything. Just her hand, firmly guiding mine to that spot.

They sit on the table, the tailors do. At least, they used to. A street of dim shops in Belgrade where we went to have my father's coat narrowed and shortened so it would fit me. The tailor got off the table and stuck pins in my shoulder. "Don't squirm," my mother said. Outside it was getting dark. Large snowflakes fell.

Years later in New York, on the same kind of afternoon, a dry-cleaning store window with an ugly, thick-legged woman on the chair in a white dress. She's having the hem raised by a gray-headed Jewish tailor, who kneels before her as if he is proposing marriage.

There was an expensive-looking suitcase on the railroad tracks, and they were afraid to come near it. Far from any station, on a stretch

254

of track bordered by orchards where they had been stealing plums that afternoon. The suitcase, she remembers, had colorful labels, of what were probably world-famous hotels and ocean liners. During the War, of course, one heard of bombs, special ones, in the shape of toys, pens, soccer balls, exotic birds—so why not suitcases? For that reason they left it where it was.

"I always wondered what was in it," my wife says. We were talking about the summer of 1944, of which we both had only a few clear recollections.

The world was going up in flames and I was studying violin. The baby Nero sawing away . . .

My teacher's apartment was always cold. A large, almost empty room with a high ceiling already in shadow. I remember the first few screechy notes my violin would make and my teacher's stern words of reprimand. I was terrified of that old woman. I also loved her because after the scolding she would give me something to eat. Something rare and exotic, like chocolate filled with sweet liqueur. We'd sit in that big empty room, almost dark now. I'd be eating and she'd be watching me eat. "Poor child," she'd say, and I thought it had to do with my not practicing enough, my being dim-witted when she tried to explain something to me, but today I'm not sure that's what she meant. In fact, I suspect she had something else entirely in mind. That's why I am writing this, to find out what it was.

When my grandfather was dying from diabetes, when he had already had one leg cut off at the knee and they were threatening to do the same to the other, his old buddy, Savo Lozanic, used to visit him every morning to keep him company. They would reminisce about this and that and even have a few laughs.

One morning my grandmother had to leave him alone in the house, as she had to attend the funeral of a distant relative. That's what gave him the idea. He hopped out of bed and into the kitchen, where he found candles and matches. He got back into his bed, somehow placed one candle above his head and the other at his feet, and lit them. Finally he pulled the sheet over his face and began to wait.

When his friend knocked, there was no answer. The door being unlocked, he went in, calling from time to time. The kitchen was empty. A fat gray cat slept on the dining room table. When he entered the bedroom and saw the bed with the sheet and lit candles, he let out a wail and then broke into sobs as he groped for a chair to sit down.

"Shut up, Savo," my grandfather said sternly from under his sheet. "Can't you see I'm only practicing?"

I leave the dentist's chair after what seems an eternity. It's an evening in June. I'm walking the tree-lined streets full of dark, whispering trees in my neighborhood in Belgrade. The streets are poorly lit, but here are people about strolling close to each other as if they were lovers. The thought crosses my mind that this is the happiest moment in my life.

In Chicago, in the 1950's, there was still an old woman with a street organ and monkey. She turned the crank with both hands while the monkey went around with a tin cup. It was some vaguely familiar tune that made our grandmothers sigh in their youth.

The woman looked like she must've known the cow that started The Great Fire. Later she married an Italian with a street organ. At times he kissed her with the monkey still on his shoulder.

The animal I saw looked young and full of mischief. He wore a tattered coat with brass buttons, which he must have inherited from his father. That day they had for an audience a small boy who wanted one of the monkey's bells. His beautiful mother kept pulling his arm to go, but he wouldn't budge. The old woman turning the crank had her eyes raised to heaven in a manner favored by saints who are being tempted by demons.

Another story about time. This one about the time it took them to quit their cells after beginning to suspect that the Germans were gone. In that huge prison in Milan all of a sudden you could hear a pin drop. Eventually they thought it best to remove their shoes before walking out.

My father was still tiptoeing hours later crossing a large empty piazza. There was a full moon above the dark palaces. His heart was in his mouth.

"It was just like an opera stage," he says. "All lit up, but nobody in the audience, and nobody in the orchestra pit. Nevertheless, I felt like singing. Or perhaps screaming?"

He did neither. The year was 1944.

The streets are empty, it's raining, and we are sitting in the Hotel Sherman bar listening to the bluesy piano. I'm not yet old enough to order a drink, but my father's presence is so authoritative and intimidating that when he orders for me the waiters never dare to ask about my age.

We talk. My father remembers a fly that wouldn't let him sleep one summer afternoon fifty years ago. I tell him about an old gray overcoat twice my size, which my mother made me wear after the War. It was wintertime. People on the street would sometimes stop and watch me. The overcoat trailed the ground and made walking difficult. One day I was standing on the corner waiting to cross when a young woman gave me a small coin and walked away. I was so embarrassed.

"Was she pretty?" my father asks.

"Not at all," I tell him. "She looked like a hick, maybe a nun."

"A Serbian Ophelia," my father thinks.

It's possible. Anything is possible.

The huge crowd cheering the dictator; the smiling faces of children offering flowers in welcome. How many times have I seen that? And always the same blonde little girl curtsying! Here she is surrounded by the high boots of the dignitaries and a couple of tightly leashed police dogs. The monster himself is patting her on the head and whispering in her ear.

I look in vain for someone with a troubled face.

The exiled general's grandson was playing war with his cheeks puffed to imitate bombs exploding. The grim daughter wrote down the old man's reminiscences. The whole apartment smelled of bad cooking.

The general was in a wheelchair. He wore a bib and smoked a cigar. The daughter smiled for me and my mother in a way that made her sharp little teeth show.

I liked the general better. He remembered some prime minister pretending to wipe his ass with a treaty he had just signed, the captured enemy officers drinking heavily and toasting some cabaret singer from their youth.

It's your birthday. The child you were appears on the street wearing a stupid grin. He wants to take you by the hand, but you won't let him.

"You've forgotten something," he whispers. And you, quiet as a mutt around an undertaker, since, of course, he (the child) doesn't exist.

There was an old fellow at the *Sun Times*, who was boss when I first came and worked as a mail clerk, who claimed to have read everything. His father was a janitor at the university library in Urbana, and Stanley, for that was his name, started as a kid. At first

I didn't believe any of it; then I asked him about Gide, whom I was then reading. He recited for me the names of the major novels and their plots. What about Isaac Babel, Alain Fournier, Aldous Huxley, Ford Madox Ford? The same thing. It was amazing! Everything I had read or heard of he had already read. "You should be on a quiz show, Stanley," people who overheard us said. Stanley had never been to college and had worked for the papers most of his life. He had a stutter, so I guess that explains why he never married or got ahead. So, all he did was read books. I had the impression that he loved every book he read. Only superlatives for Stanley, one book better than the other. If I started to criticize, he'd get pissed off. Who do I think I am? Smartass, he called me, and wouldn't talk to me about books for a few days. Stanley was pure enthusiasm. I was giddy myself at the thought of another book waiting for me to read at home.

In Chicago there was a tremendous suspicion of the Eastern literary establishment. The working people never get portrayed in their books, I heard people say all the time. Most of the people I met were leftist intellectuals from working-class and immigrant backgrounds. These were Jews, Poles, Germans, Irish. They had relatives who worked in factories. They knew America could be a cruel place, an unjust country. After I saw South Chicago and Gary, Indiana, I had to admit they had a point. Both places, with their steel mills in smoke and fire, were like hell out of Hieronymus Bosch. The ugliness and poverty of industrial Chicago was an enormous influence on me. It prevented me from forgetting where I came from. A big temptation for all immigrants with intellectual pretensions is to outdo the natives in their love of Henry James and whatever he represents. You want to blend in, so you're always looking for the role models. It's very understandable. Who wants to look and talk like a foreigner forever!

JEFFREY SKINNER
Salt Water Amnesia (2005)

Jeffrey Skinner is the author of four previous books of poetry. His poems, plays and stories have gathered grants, fellowships, and awards from such sources as the National Endowment for the Arts, the Ingram Merrill Foundation, the Howard Foundation, and the state arts agencies of Connecticut, Delaware, and Kentucky. He has been awarded residencies at Yaddo, McDowell, and the Fine Arts Center in Provincetown. His work has been featured numerous times on National Public Radio. Skinner is President of the Board of Directors, and Editorial Consultant, for Sarabande Books, a literary publishing house he founded with his wife Sarah Gorham.

In his own words: "I would like to be the genetically engineered love child of Zbigniew Herbert and Dylan Thomas. That is, I would like to write poetry that has the philosophical ease and metaphoric inventiveness of the Eastern Europeans, *and* at the same time sings like a drunken Welshman. I would prefer it if my poems were a bit closer to speech on the *elevation* —> <—*speech* spectrum; I'm very fond of the casual talk of our time. And I would like to include a variety of tones and structural strategies—dead serious and slapstick, formal and 'free.' I want the thrill of victory *and* the agony of defeat. I want to include that poor bastard they showed wiping out in slow motion on the ski jump every Sunday afternoon.

We all want to know why the universe is the way it is and not otherwise. Or why it is at all. Poetry is my way of putting such questions and going outside for a walk. It's good for all kinds of weather, for the country as well as the city. When I'm inside poetry I seem compelled to enter the ocean, or an idea, or a city I once knew, or my cruelty, or whatever—without lying. Poetry seems to have something to do with attention; and with love, if one can say such a thing without getting all wet. But what that something is, I don't know."

THE COLT

In the field and everywhere I am never far from mother.
Mother covers my face with her tail and the brightness of sky
is split. When there is danger mother puts her body
between me and danger. In the center of the field an island
of trees fenced in. Why an island of trees fenced in?
Sometimes I must rear up suddenly in the wind
and run, fast, so that all my mind is running
and then I don't care about danger and I am glad
for the fence or else I would never stop. Tired now
of maintaining this poem in the voice of a young horse
I rise and walk out: enormous brain, wobbling on toothpicks.

MY DATES

On a long beach walk in winter I transcended my envy. The cold white spray of breakers starched it out. By the time I reached the rocky point of Misquamicut I could think of no one with whom I would trade fortunes. In fact I did not think, only sat on a boulder below the tide line and looked down at surf slapping the boulder's hard skirt, as if the ocean might climb up and convert me to the Church of Holy Liquidity. I was beautifully inhuman, and don't remember the feel of my own body. The ocean's single-minded dedication made sense, tumbling smooth and small the rocks and wood and hunks of glass. Dead life too was converted, into darting bodies, rubbery shapes. The sea: professional, gray, unhurried. Heavy as lead one day, translucent lime floating beneath the air the next.

The bad news: I began to envy the ocean, which I realized had already outlived me countless times, and in all those lifetimes never stopped coming, violent and fresh as birth, slamming down without discrimination on the grit or rock-plane shore, wood glass rock or bone. It seemed to have both immortal soul and body. It buried its dead and then began the resurrection at once—same place, same time. From the beginning humans came to worship the waves and the sea's stubborn indifference to beauty. As I walked, I gradually regained the hard borders of human form. When I got home everything was the same. I was again afraid of death, or rather, afraid of immensities that lay on either side of my consciousness: my dates, separated by a dash. The dash, unmoving.

THE LONG MARRIAGE

They could not believe their luck – sunlight all the way down, lighting rocks lodged in the sandy bottom as if from within. Each rock angled just so, by some immense but casual intelligence. Rock weed held out its dark green fingers, waving. How can the water be so clear, and full of salt? In between their visits someone had removed the used condoms and shattered beer glass from the concrete cubicles, the breakwater fronting the old factory. *The olfactory*, he said. She did not see the humor.

At the beach a group gathered around the harbor seal who had hauled herself a small way onto the shore, waving an aristocratic flipper in the sun. Can't a mammal have a bit of privacy? She knew the feeling. The vertebra he plucked from the sand and showed her proudly was smooth, and cleanest white. But she would not have it in the house. Be happy you are alive and moving, she said. Bones belong in the sand, rocks on ocean floor, and mercy in the great, shadowy hands of the indifferent one.

THEORY OF THE WOUNDED HEN

Simone Weil's mind leapt, from those few friends she had allowed close enough to harm her, to the wounded hen attacked by other animals in the yard. Such savagery was not evil, she insisted—only mechanical. She forgave. As to real food she ate what the poorest consumed during wartime, and thus drove herself to her own "de-creation." This was mysterious, but expected—at five she had allowed herself no more than the amount of sugar rationed to each soldier. Her life fit snugly between two wars. Still, the word *de-creation*, like a tack in the shoe . . . What did the workers at the Renault plant make of this Jewish-looking woman who prayed like a Catholic, and lectured them on the Upanishads? How did she know the mind of a wounded hen?

THE SINGER

This morning I began with large ambition to write a love poem. Give me a sonnet, I prayed, that captures my longing for the beloved. After all, I *do* love, I'm sure of it. But as soon as I wrote one line I saw how instantly familiar it was: the words in an order they had known before, in someone else's life, from someone else's mouth. It wasn't mine. When I crossed that line out and tried to begin again, no words came. Instead, my mind filled with an image of Rosemary Clooney, singing "They Can't Take That Away From Me." I'd seen the clip on TV the night before, because Rosemary had just died, after a long and brilliant career that included—as they say in Hollywood—bouts of addiction and depression. Rosemary was huge, she looked like a circus tent with a head poking through the top. She was singing, but, really, she was dead.

MY GENERATION ABHORRED LIMITS

So it's pleasing to think of an infinite number
of alternate universes: branches of a tree diverging from one trunk,
all swaying greenly in their slightly varying prospects
on sun and wind and the daily traffic. But in fact
I did not accept the offer to sell airplane parts out of Chicago,
which would've made me a rich man. I did not
urge Elizabeth to keep the child. And you did not choose
the other poet with his hand on your knee
under a table the three of us shared. For love, you turned
down the gig in Chapel Hill. And when we look over
our shoulder now, the spaces we saw as open air
are occupied, each choice inscribed in matter,
pith to bundle scar: as it happened, once, for all time.

BLACK OLIVES

I take my father for an interview with Jesus, who has rented temporary headquarters in a cave. My father is not very mobile, so I have to carry him in pieces, one piece at a time over the dusty heat of the stones. Jesus is there, sitting cross-legged on a rug, eating black olives.

My father laboriously reassembles himself in the silence. Suddenly Jesus is next to him, placing an olive on his lips. The olive glints wetly in the cave light. Then, I remember: olives are one of the foods my father hates. I look away, hoping he does not say something to insult Our Lord.

When I look back it's just me and dad. I manipulate his arms and legs, turn his creaky head 360 degrees. And, hell: he seems no better than before. But then I lift my father and he is light, light enough to carry in one piece, and the evening air has cooled the stones, and the scent of myrrh trails down from a gigantic moon.

IMPATIENS IN DROUGHT

Flowering plant spread like a fan
from the window box
a hundred exhausted red faces pressing outward
immigrants from a boat stopped short
of shore by coastal agents

realize only now too late
the green tether that feeds us also
holds us back, o mirage, o my longing

SAM TAYLOR
Body of the World (2005)

Sam Taylor recently lived for several years in Northern New Mexico, where he was the caretaker for a snowed-in wilderness refuge without phone or electricity. He is currently comparatively plugged in within a country cabin in Virginia. In 2006, he was awarded the Dobie Paisano Fellowship from the Texas Institute of Letters. Recent work appears in the *New Republic, Crab Orchard Review, Orion, Agni,* and *Green Mountains Review.*

In his own words: "I don't believe anyone 'writes' a poem. The poet does work, however, and somewhere in this work participates with the birth of something new and the arrival of something already existent. I was not consciously working on a book during this time— just poems. Nevertheless, the book is unified by my concerns of the period. Written in the time I was 19 to 28, the poems in *Body of the World* explore the world as the self—one of the perennial themes of mysticism—and wrestle with the suffering and violence such a unified vision must confront and subsume. Sometimes late at night, when I almost forget 'I' wrote the book, I enjoy reading it."

ARC

As it is given, it is whispered, it shall be lost.
It begins with your name
and the marble block that becomes your face.
It begins with a city
where your cry is small as the seeds of coriander.

It begins with a claw foot bath and a wind of pine,
mother's black hair,
a flickering streetlight, the waxy yellow skin
of starfruit, and sneaking in
to read your father's manuscript. It begins with seeing a movie

and walking out into a storm. Then everything speeds up.
A jackhammer, lunch counters,
people like a million pebbles, airports, orchids,
dental floss. And soon
you have forgotten that the world is new.

And in the middle, you will be a two piece suit
between traffic signals,
but in the end, the underside of ambrosia
and the breath of green tea.
In the middle, women will come to you naked

with hair clips given to them by their grandmothers,
a sari from the Indian coast,
a limp from when they fell running through the park.
You will watch them try on shoes,
and you will wash them with a vanishing bar of oatmeal soap.

It begins with one woman on a stone bench waiting
beneath a sycamore.
Her body will be filled with torn photographs,
and you will carry them in
and out of Texacos, piece them together by fluorescent light.

When she leaves, it will be because of a complex equation,
a calculus that includes
measurements of how the barges lift the bay, the change
at dusk in children's pockets,
angles of first hallways, additions and subtractions

of plovers, sandpipers. Or something simple and inscrutable
as the surface of a circle—
the digits of pi will follow her down unrepeating streets
past crates of oranges, gaping
mouths of fish, into other rooms, books that you will never read.

Then there will be strangers, elevators, stones scattered in
indoor hotel gardens.
The giant green wings of luna moths, a broom, dust. Maybe
another, hands like
obsolete maps, maybe children, small moons that seem to wane

as your light fades, swallowed into the texture of hay bales,
into the coffee mug light,
the banana leaf light, you will wash the knives, chop cedar. The
sun will keep setting
deeper in your flesh. And the dark,
the dark light. As it leaves, it will whisper, I was never yours.

HOLOGRAM

When you are sailing and the wind on your brow
makes your outside feel like a blue heart,
don't forget that it's dark inside your pocket
and that the pocket watch that is not there
lies under a glass window in downtown Houston
where a Mexican boy thinks of his grandfather,
points, asks how much it costs. Don't forget
he breakdances in the evening at the Y
and the girl in the corner who just watches
and says "Miguel, you're not using your shoulder"
is also watching you as you suddenly stand
feeling brittle as the cliffs, and so small
a hawk could drag you off. But the girl is happy
to feel the wind on your arm and know there is no end
to the commas in the blue scripture,
though she thinks more often of whether
her parents will be watching television
or fighting when she gets home that night
and of whether or not she is pretty.

ACCIDENT

A beacon moving through the darkest crime scene
my friend said when I told him I didn't know
what love was. Two months later, Joel woke up
reclined in a truck that had no doors or windshield,
his left shoe missing, the driver's seat beside him
empty. Somebody was calling his name—

no, not his name, just calling him, so precisely
it tugged his sternum like a name. He rose,
walked around the vehicle—the tires
were gone, two wheels stripped to their axles—
and there she was on the ground, sitting
against the truck, legs outstretched. He felt relieved,

she must have collapsed, pouting at herself,
sheepish for the mess she'd caused. Where was the road?
He heard it humming in the distance. He leaned down
to her, but she did not move. He was terrified then
of the silence he felt that moment
which was not the quiet of trees or the moon

or of hot tea, but the silence of somewhere else,
of a lake being where a girl should be.
I didn't ask him if he saw a beacon in that field,
the windshield shattered sixty yards away,
the sky a frigid wishing well. I imagine
what he would have to say—waking in the twisted metal

dark, walking round the Ford to find her
sitting in the grass, already gone, her suitcase open
fifty feet away. That there was no beacon, just taillights
and windows scattered in the weeds, the truck's steel carcass,
and the stars they had shared, now his alone,
tickling her shell. The beacon was nowhere. He was the beacon

he would have to say, standing alone, his pulse snapping
against the sky, filling the veins of the night,
plasma, cartilage, bone—crying out for her,
her jacket flapping in the bush. He would have to say
that love does not mean preservation alone,
but also creation and destruction, and only then

is a thing complete, is it revealed, like the windshield
shattered sixty yards away, like Somayyah dead,
sitting calmly in the grass, after the truck she crashed
flipped over fifteen times. Some things are impossible
and they come true. Maybe all things. Two days later,
he returned to the road, found a two inch groove

that trailed into the scrub, followed it, picking up
his wallet, a cell phone, her water bottle. A letter
he had written her last summer, half rain-bled. The truck
towed and gone, he found her spilled menstrual pads
still caught in the sumac, left them, sobbing. I imagine
what he would have to say: that there is no thing

that is not a beacon. No thing that is not a flag
in a mute's hand, trying to reach us. Or a window
holding a face. Except in some spots, the face shines through
more than others, like in Somayyah alive,
or like that night as he leaned over her, noticing
her left foot in the grass was bare, like his own,

and two days later—when his father drove him back—
he found, on a sun-washed hill, beneath a tall pine
her boot, standing upright, still laced and tied.

JOHN 3:16

"For God so loved the world, he gave his only Son. . ."

The perfection of God that rose
        Jesus out of its body also put forth
two Mexican girls, four and five, running alone
        down a city street, a wind of white dresses
and red ribbons, hair as fine as black water—
        shouts leaping halfway down the block—
then the mother rounding the corner
        behind them, shaking her head, "They wore me out."

A streak of laughter now. But it could be
        one day mother will be roasting corn
and an uncle will lead one of the girls
        behind a shed—a birthday present he says—

and before she knows how to braid her hair
        or ever hears of Shakespeare, she will tear
her face to shrapnel in the mirror, follow
        any boy who curses down an alley.

That's why he's on the cross. Not for one sin
        or another, but to show us the nature
of birth, to tell himself—his children—the price
        of existence. Because God so loved the world,

he wanted to be a girl with red ribbons,
        a blue Minnie Mouse watch, even if then
he had to forget, to live amongst all the forgetting—
        the tv talk show, the uncle, to watch him each day
through the smell of corn. Because He so loved the world,
        he was willing even to be that fat man

lying on the couch eating *chicharones*,
                    scratching his balls, chafed red from the quarry,
because the white light just goes on forever.

CODA: FOR WHOM THE BELL TOLLS

Where is the doorway into this impure world?
We are currently experiencing a high volume of calls.
When he turns the faucet on, her blood begins to flow,
the man who lives below them starts to sing.

All morning, the mourning dove. All mourning, the morning.
Your call will be answered in the order it was received.
The bureau of your chest filled with last year's papers;
there are words from here to the end of the world.

So reach out a lace of poplar across a dark continent.
When she turns the wipers on, the sky begins to fall.
Look out the window at one version of mystery.
Who then has lived up to the dignity of a hand?

If you see a woman climbing stairs forever, ignore her.
A wicker laundry basket overflowing with primary hues.
If the stairs are made of metal, if you see her pause
and glance at you, unsung arias condensed to stone, pass on.

Do not worry. The woman changes. She is renewed.
And ask not for what reason she looks at you.
This message will now be repeated twice.
You may exit at any time by pressing zero.

BRUCE WEIGL
Declension in the Village of Chung Luong (2006)

Bruce Weigl is the author of more than a dozen books of poetry, several translations, and the best-selling memoir *The Circle of Hanh*. He has been awarded many honors, including the Paterson Poetry Prize, Fellowships from the National Endowment for the Arts and the Yaddo Foundation, two Pushcart Prizes, and the Poet's Prize from the Academy of American Poets. Weigl lives in Oberlin, Ohio.

In his own words: "The presence of death ... plays a very important role not just in the poetry of Keats and Wordsworth and Coleridge, but in the way they saw the world, and ultimately lived their lives. They believed that the fierce beauty of our lives existed only because of the inevitability of our deaths. The fact that we all die is why our lives are beautiful. But what I learned from Keats ... is that what the presence of our imminent deaths calls for is a more ironic regard for our lives: an openness to possibility instead of a devotion to failure ... Two things happen simultaneously in the writer's life: as you work more and more and get older, you begin to recognize more and more the enormous possibilities at hand, and at the same time your own human limitations. That's another one of those wonderful paradoxes that leads us to poetry I think. That, and the fact that your first responsibility as a writer is to recognize the inherent failure of language to say a thing straight." —from an interview with David Keplinger in *War, Literature & the Arts: An International Journal of the Humanities* published by the English Department at the U.S. Air Force Academy.

SAY GOOD-BYE

Say river. Say bloody current. Say not enough rice.
      Say mother and father. Say village bell calling.
Say village drum calling. Say music through the trees

      from someone's lonely radio. Say mango
sliced into the woman's open hands.
      Say rice, steaming just in time. Say paths

worn by the naked feet of lovers. Say lovers
      who must hide in the mango groves,
even to say good-bye.

PORTAL

In our hallucination, the children are instructed
in the ways of finding shelter
when the rain of our bombs comes down
on their small villages and schools. The children
can identify our planes, and
what our planes can do to them. They

sleep the sleep of weary warriors
beaten down and left for nothing in their lonely deaths
that come so slowly you would wish
your own heart empty of blood.
I watched the people gather in the street
to stop the war that is the war against ourselves,
against the children who practice finding our planes
before they're blown up into dust
nobody sees, but that
makes a sound like the vanquished.

EDDY

My friend Eddy had a younger brother who
definitely had something fucked up in his brain. Eddy's mother
prayed out loud all day in her bedroom, lit with candles.
I never heard his solemn, steel mill father
utter one single syllable. Not ever.

Because no one else would, I loved Eddy. I went to his house
where other children feared to go. I heard his mother
pray and weep so loud, I almost ran away
until Eddy held my wrist and said to take it slow.
I didn't know then what immaculate beauties I was among.

We tried to teach his brother how to use a fork and spoon;
how to zip his fly and pee like a man;
how to swing the bat, but he never learned,
and I didn't know then
that love could be about two boys like that,

or that what Eddy held fast before the waves of prayer,
and the stony father's silence,
and the world's infinite
indignities, is called brother,
and what he gave up, is called everything.

THE ABANDONMENT OF BEAUTY
AT ALLEN MEMORIAL HOSPITAL

When the polite, almost noiseless doctors
invited Mr. Death into our conversation, my heart sang out.
Not from their words,
because words make you accountable;
they said it with their grim countenance,
and with the weight of their bodies in the space we shared.
I could see Mr. Death
appear in a corner of the midnight window,
and though he would not come into the light,
I knew he had his eye on me.
Oh where was beauty when I needed it.
How it turned away;
how it had loved me though my life like no one else,
then in the end meant nothing.

MY UNCLE RUDY IN SUNLIGHT

Out of the hole my father and his brother had dug
below the drainage tiles of my uncle's barn,
        hundreds of mice streamed.
These brothers had dug the hole,
        then snaked a hose deep into the nest the mice had made,
and no way out but one. They had started getting bad,
        and when my aunt found them in her pantry, well,
something had to be done. I was five years old, and I
        stood behind these brave men and watched
between their legs as the mice began to come:
        first, only a few, shaking the water from their fur, blinded
momentarily in sunlight, and then, may I say, a flood of mice;
        more mice than anyone had expected, even I knew that.
My uncle had a hoe, and my father ran for the rake,
        and you know what happens next.

This was fifty years ago, and I don't know
what business it thinks it has here, in this life, now.
        Yet in the dizzying span of memory,
that morning in the country of mice is as clear to me
        as my own face, which I love,
and as clear as the face of my uncle ,
        moving in and out of the blinding sun as he raised the hoe,
and then came down hard, and then raised the hoe again.

DECLENSION IN THE VILLAGE
OF CHUNG LUONG

The dark is so dark in the northern countryside.
No city lights, few
        cars, mostly oil lamps and small fires for cooking,
by which you can see the faces of living people.
            In the afternoon, I had watched some small boys
bathe and swim and play
        in the clay-colored water of this village pond,
where only they may swim, and never a girl.
            Beyond the pond,
beyond the three churches in the village, beyond the school,
        and the teacher's house, beyond the endless fields of rice,
the river valley opens up into a kingdom
        whose river is as red as the patriots' blood.
Red as the blood of the comrade,
        dead where she waited for her lover
in the mango grove;
        dead by the hand of the puppet soldiers
who shoot in the back
        so you may not see their face. Loss
is a red thread, woven into the cloth of the woman's shawl; grief
        is the knot that binds it.

LESSON FROM DA LAT

        We love emptiness
because reason is useless.

        The boy carries his cricket in a box his grandfather
had constructed with heart-breaking

care from tiny splinters of bamboo.
        He carries it in his satchel with the ball of sticky rice

his mother had wrapped for him in a banana leaf, for his lunch,
        in the still dark morning while he slept.

He walks to school
        with his friends through the mango trees,

the guardians of wandering beings
        everywhere.

LATE SUMMER LILIES

  I kiss the late summer lilies because they want me to,
and how do you say no to lilies
   dying of beauty you can barely stand to see.
I don't know if I heard a voice or not, or anything at all,
    except the dangerous wind. Nothing else to say

    in this great Republic of Voices, this Republic of Lies.
Into the darkness to see I was called,
    and to taste the salty flesh,
and to suck sweet juice from the lilies, holes in the sky
    moving away from us like nothing we've ever seen.

KAREN WHALLEY
The Rented Violin (2003)

Karen Whalley's work has appeared in many literary journals, including *Harvard Review, Blue Unicorn, Passages North, Bellowing Ark,* and *Shades.* In 2001 she was the recipient of a Rona Jaffe Award for Poetry. She has taught English at Peninsula College, and currently lives and works in Port Townsend, Washington. *The Rented Violin* is her first book.

In her own words: "*The Rented Violin* was written over a period of seven years, at a time when I was in the process of profound changes in my life precipitated by a painful divorce. I think the book attempts to orient me to the outer world in a new way, while taking into account the personal history of family and how that has shaped me. So, there are multiple layers of experience occurring in the poems, a mutual exchange between the world and me that leaves both the world and myself altered through the writing of the poems. I think the book reflects the failures of love, either in my own life or the lives of strangers. Yet, I would say that hope in the poems is the ability to accept love as failure, but also as redemption."

YELLOW FROM A DISTANCE

We have almost reached the pond;
You have left your glasses at home on the table
And squint across the field
To the unfolding skunk cabbage.
Farsighted or near, I can't remember which
But you say it is only yellow you see
Which from a distance could be daffodils.
But they are different shapes, the bell and the candle,
And I describe to you how they float
On the marsh like a harbor of lanterns,
Because I want you to see them as I do,
A thousand tiny sails, each distinct,
Each one among the others, each drifting.

To you, the world's a blur, and I recall another walk
When the cherry trees had lifted their pink awnings
And you couldn't see the trees themselves,
Only the row of cloudy blossoms passing overhead—
Happy for that much. I think sometimes
You leave them off,
Not because you love my voice
As we pass each yard with its scrubby patch of flowers,
Or how I tell the shades of blue,
But because the earth is beautiful
And beauty is a form of suffering.

HOLLYHOCKS

The moment a man questions
The meaning of his life, he is sick.
                        —Sigmund Freud

I don't remember when I stopped
Questioning. Maybe it was when
My neighbor Marge lost her daughter
To cancer, buried without her hair.
Marge didn't mention it
When she carried a bowl
Of cherry tomatoes over
And stood in the cidery shade
Of a small-leafed tree, not talking
Across the fence. *This heat's blinding,*
She said, and held a long salute
Above her eyes, twisting her sad
Gray braid into a knot at the nape.
Why didn't she say something?

I look a little foolish as I look
Back now, standing waist-deep in yarrow,
Happy as a hat, checking for leaf miners,
As if we both had time enough
To speculate the way we did
On what color you'd call the hollyhocks.
As if pink weren't enough of a word.
Maybe what she needed
When the call came from Idaho
Was to pick a bowl of cold tomatoes.

Maybe she needed to be
Any old woman in the world but her
Stooping to tall hollyhocks
And searching her mind
For just the right shade of pink.

FRENCH ROSE

It is the day after Thanksgiving,
The year terrorists
Toppled two buildings in the name of religion
And gave Americans the gift
Of humility and took from them a certain innocence.
It is the year
In which I fell out of love—
Or he fell out of love with me,
Which is really the long angel's fall
From grace, from the heaven
A good feeling makes between two people,
And I learned redemption
Is passing up the opportunity
To stay in pain.

I am watching the apple tree
Drop precisely one apple per day,
As if it has mastered the beautiful art
Of giving up, and in that nudity
It is free of red ornaments
Like the vulnerable face
Of a woman without lipstick
Who has made her peace
With the pretenses of the world.

I am poor, and single.
I am poor and married
To the idea of happiness, the same way *sky*
Is the only word for *blue*.
Because it's my birthday,
I bathed this morning
In the French rose soap
My sister bought for me
At a ritzy store in an upscale mall
Proving there is a world
Where people care about the way things smell
And the delicate, carved *M*
In the top of the bar
Like a secret initial to some exclusive club
So that a woman like myself
Might rise one morning
From the sweet and steamy bath
Into cold November air,
Slick and pink from the hot water
Ready to begin again with a faith
Odd as a terrorist's, thinking, *This is how you live, this
Is what you do.*

LAZARUS

By March, the leaves are budding
On the dogwood; the bulb species
Is resurrecting in tight green scrolls.

Gardens aren't natural: what I mean is,
Someone had to put them there. Someone
Carried a basket through a nursery

And chose from among the many plants,
This violet, say, for its lacy flowers,
This tulip for its flagrant, lipstick red.

So many others left on the shelf,
Like books you'll never get to read,
Or like the puppy at the pound

Whose large paws foretold
A future of uncontainable joy
For which your house felt too small.

In this way, only, we resemble God,
Deciding what goes and what stays
As the water rises around us,

Which is our life going under.
For instance, this morning
I dug last year's perennial geranium

From the ground to put in a meadow rue.
That quickly, desire had changed
Something already good into something

Not much better, which is enough,
Almost, to make me satisfied
With what I already have,

Which is spring and this feeling
Like sinking, that nothing ever ends
And that nothing ever lasts.

BELOW ZERO

At night, in the warm pipes
Beneath the house, in the dark tunnels
Under the iron grids of the vents,
A small soft body claws.

It moves from one end of the bedroom
To the other, neither fast nor furious
But trapped. I imagine a mouse,
A rat maybe, burrowed up through some small
Opening expecting to find food or nest
Or a field leading to others of its kind,
But I am not its kind.

By morning, it is gone
The floorboards beneath me empty
And only the clock's audible increments
Of time pushing me forward from stove
To sink to dishes and, at last, my desk
Where, relieved in this bright light
There is nothing I have to kill or to save.

THE CALLING

It lit above me
On the top rail of the fence,
An ordinary sparrow
Startling the silence. It fixed a grave eye on me,
Contemplative and curious,
As just that morning I'd watched
A knotted worm untangle itself
From the dirt. *Five inches*
Is as a thousand years of effort,
Said the Buddha of my soul,
While I chipped at the ground with a trowel
And listened to his song.

He saw a pile of green
On the green grass as I plucked weeds
From the green thicket of montbretia.
He saw that I was moving
This green to *that* green
With great care and consideration.

And he cocked his head and shivered
And told me to rise up
And look at what I'd done.
I don't remember whether it was his word
Or mine, but the self
Inside my head was stunned
That my life had made no difference.

C.K. WILLIAMS
Love About Love; Selected Love Poems (2000)

C. K. Williams is the author of many books of poetry, including *Repair,* which won the 2000 Pulitzer Prize and the *Los Angeles Times* Book Award. He has won many other awards, including the Ruth Lilly Prize, the National Book Award, and the National Book Critics Circle Award. He teaches at Princeton University and lives part of the year in France.

In his own words: "Human beings experience ourselves as assemblages, almost collages, of the passionate, the sensual, the intellectual and the spiritual. We are at once philosophers, aestheticians, social and political theorists; we are lovers and haters, children and parents, we lie, we tell the truth, we make myths and stories; there is violence in us, which is our evolutionary inheritance, but there is also the unlikely charity which illuminates so much of our spiritual history. And what's more, we are both participants and observers of all these portions of ourselves, these selves. Poetry's real greatness is that it is the most effective means we have of bringing together these apparently disparate parts of ourselves. Because to be real poetry must be true, and because it must deal unconditionally with the reality of a single person's existence, by its definition it entails a bringing together of selves within the self. Poetry makes us more whole than we ever thought we could be."

YOURS

I'd like every girl in the world to have a poem of her own
I've written for her I don't even want to make love to them all
    anymore
just write things your body makes me delirious your face enchants me
you are a wonder of soul spirit intelligence one for every one
and then the men I don't care whether I can still beat them all
them too a poem for them how many?
seeing you go through woods like part of the woods seeing you play
    piano
seeing you hold your child in your tender devastating hands
and of course the children too little poems they could sing or dance to
this is our jumping game this our seeing game our holding each other
even the presidents with all their death the congressmen and judges
I'd give them something
they would hold awed to their chests as their proudest life thing
somebody walking along a road where there's no city would look up
and see his poem coming down like a feather out of nowhere
or on the assembly line new instructions a voice sweet as lunch-time
or she would turn over a stone by the fire and if she couldn't read
it would sing to her in her body
listen! everyone! you have your own poem now
it's yours as much as your heart as much as your own life is
you can do things to it shine it up iron it dress it in doll clothes
o men! o people! please stop how it's happening now please
I'm working as fast as I can I can't stop to use periods
sometimes I draw straight lines on the page because the words
are too slow
I can only do one at a time don't die first please
don't give up and start crying or hating each other they're coming
I'm hurrying be patient there's still time isn't there? isn't there?

THE GAS STATION

This is before I'd read Nietzsche. Before Kant or Kierkegaard,
     even before Whitman and Yeats.
I don't think there were three words in my head yet. I knew, perhaps,
     that I should suffer,
I can remember I almost cried for this or for that, nothing special,
     nothing to speak of.
Probably I was mad with grief for the loss of my childhood, but I
     wouldn't have known that.
It's dawn. A gas station. Route twenty-two. I remember exactly:
     route twenty-two curved,
there was a squat, striped concrete divider they'd put in after a
     plague of collisions.
The gas station? Texaco, Esso—I don't know. They were just words
     anyway then, just what their signs said.
I wouldn't have understood the first thing about monopoly or
     imperialist or oppression.
It's dawn. It's so late. Even then, when I was never tired, I'm just
     holding on.
Slumped on my friend's shoulder, I watch the relentless, wordless
     misery of the route twenty-two sky
that seems to be filming my face with a grainy oil I keep trying to
     rub off or in.
Why are we here? Because one of my friends, in the men's room over
     there, has blue balls.
He has to jerk off. I don't know what that means, "blue balls," or why
     he has to do that—
it must be important to have to stop here after this long night, but I
     don't ask.
I'm just trying, I think, to keep my head as empty as I can for as long
     as I can.

One of my other friends is asleep. He's so ugly, his mouth hanging,
    slack and wet.
Another—I'll never see this one again—stares from the window
    as though he were frightened.
Here's what we've done. We were in Times Square, a pimp found
    us, corralled us, led us somewhere,
down a dark street, another dark street, up dark stairs, dark hall,
    dark apartment,
where his whore, his girl or his wife or his mother for all I know
    dragged herself from her sleep
propped herself on an elbow, gazed into the dark hall, and agreed,
    for two dollars each, to take care of us.
Take care of us. Some of the words that come through me now seem
    to stay, to hook in.
My friend in the bathroom is taking so long. The filthy sky must
    be starting to lighten.
It took me a long time, too, with the woman, I mean. Did I mention
    that she, the woman, the whore or mother,
was having her time and all she would deign to do was to blow us?
    Did I say that? Deign? Blow?
What a joy, though, the idea was in those days. Blown! What a
    thing to tell the next day.
She only deigned, though, no more. She was like a machine. When
    I lift her back to me now,
there's nothing there but that dark, curly head, working, a machine,
    up and down, and now,
Freud, Marx, Fathers, tell me, what am I, doing this, telling this, on
    her, on myself,
hammering it down, cementing it, sealing it in, but a machine too?
    Why am I doing this?

I still haven't read Augustine. I don't understand Chomsky that
    well. Should I?
My friend at last comes back. Maybe the right words were there all
    along. *Complicity. Wonder.*
How pure we were then, before Rimbaud, before Blake. *Grace. Love.*
    Take care of us. Please.

LOVE: BEGINNINGS

They're at that stage where so much desire streams between them,
    so much frank need and want,
so much absorption in the other and the self and the self-admiring
    entity and unity they make—
her mouth so full, breast so lifted, head thrown back *so* far in her
    laughter at his laughter,
he so solid, planted, oaky, firm, so resonantly factual in the headiness
    of being craved so,
she almost wreathed upon him as they intertwine again, touch again,
    cheek, lip, shoulder, brow,
every glance moving toward the sexual, every glance away soaring
    back in flame into the sexual—
that just to watch them is to feel again that hitching in the groin,
    that filling of the heart,
the old, sore heart, the battered, foundered, faithful heart, snorting
    again, stamping in its stall.

THE GAME

"Water" was her answer and I fell instantly and I knew self-de-
        structively in love with her,
had to have her, would, I knew, someday, I didn't care how, and
        soon, too, have her,
though I guessed already it would have to end badly though not so
        disastrously as it did.

My answer, "lion" or "eagle," wasn't important: the truth would have
        been anything but myself.
The game of that first fateful evening was what you'd want to come
        back as after you died;
it wasn't the last life-or-death contest we'd have, only the least
        erotically driven and dangerous.

What difference if she was married, and perhaps mad (both only a
        little, I thought wrongly?)
There was only my jealous glimpse of her genius, then my vision
        of vengeance: midnight, morning—
beneath me a planet possessed: cycles of transfiguration and soaring,
        storms crossing.

REALMS

Often I have thought that after my death, not in death's void as we
usually think of it,
but in some simpler after-realm of the mind, it will be given to me
to transport myself
through all space and all history, to behold whatever and converse
with whomever I wish.

Sometimes I might be an actual presence, a traveler listening at the
edge of the crowd;
at other times I'd have no physical being; I'd move unseen but seeing
through palace or slum.
Sophocles, Shakespeare, Bach! Grandfathers! Homo-erectus! The
universe bursting into being!

Now, though, as I wake, caught by some imprecise longing, you in
the darkness beside me,
your warmth flowing gently against me, it comes to me that in all my
after-death doings,
I see myself as alone, always alone, and I'm suddenly stranded, for-
saken, desperate, lost.

To propel myself through those limitless reaches without you!
Never! Be with me, come!
Babylon, Egypt, Lascaux, the new seas boiling up life; Dante, Delphi,
Magyars and Mayans!
Wait, though, it must be actually you, not my imagination of you,
however real: for myself,
mind would suffice, no matter if all were one of time's terrible toys,
but I must have you,
as you are, the unquenchable fire of your presence, otherwise death
truly would triumph.
Quickly, never mind death, never mind mute, oblivious, onrushing
time: wake, hold me!

ARCHETYPES

Often before have our fingers touched in sleep or half-sleep and
    enlaced,
often I've been comforted through a dream by that gently sensitive
    pressure,
but this morning, when I woke your hand lay across mine in an
    awkward,
unfamiliar position so that it seemed strangely external to me,
    removed,
an object whose precise weight, volume and form I'd never remarked:
its taut, resistant skin, dense muscle-pads, the subtle, complex structure,
with delicately elegant chords of bone aligned like columns in a
    temple.

Your fingers began to move then, in brief, irregular tensions and
    releasings;
it felt like your hand was trying to hold some feathery, fleeting creature,
then you suddenly, fiercely jerked it away, rose to your hands and knees,
and stayed there, palms flat on the bed, hair tangled down over your
    face,
until with a coarse sigh, almost like a snarl you abruptly let yourself fall
and lay still, your hands drawn tightly to your chest, your head
    turned away,
forbidden to me, I thought, by whatever had raised you to that defiant
    crouch.

I waited, hoping you'd wake, turn, embrace me, but you stayed in
    yourself,
and I felt again how separate we all are from one another, how even
    our passions,

which seem to embody unities outside of time, heal only the most
    benign divisions,
that for our more abiding, ancient terrors we each have to find our
    own valor.
You breathed more softly now, though; I took heart, touched
    against you,
and, as though nothing had happened, you opened your eyes,
    smiled at me,
and murmured—how almost startling to hear you in your real
    voice—"Sleep, love."

Jonaathan Aaron *by Gaylen Morgan*
Julie Agoos *by Jeremy Paul*
Pamela Alexander *by Ed Seling*
Keith Althaus *by Susan Baker*
Craig Arnold *by Amanda Abel*
Adrian Blevins *by Julia Zhosan*
Laure-Anne Bosselaar *by Star Black*
Robert Boyers *by Emma Dodge Hanson*
Julianne Buchsbaum *by Robert Peterson*
Hayden Carruth *by Hank O'Neal*
Patrick Donnelly *by Matt Valentine*
Lilah Hegnauer *by Hannah Rae Hegnauer*
Tung-Hui Hu *by Andrew Moisey*
Linton Kwesi Johnson *by Danny DaCosta*
Laura Kasischke *by Bill Abernethy*
Gary Copeland Lilley *by Ariel Studenmund*
Khaled Mattawa *by Amanda Abel*
William Matthews *by Ted Rosenberg*
Roger Mitchell *by www.wblstudio.com*
Steve Orlen *by Gail Marcus Orlen*
Eric Pankey *by Jennifer Atkinson*
Kathleen Peirce *by Don Andrews*
Josh Rathkamp *by Joanna Robbins*
James Richardson *by Pryde Brown*
Seido Ray Ronci *by August Kryger*
Charles Simic *by The Portsmouth Herald*
Jeffrey Skinner *by Laura Skinner*
Sam Taylor *by Sam Taylor*
Bruce Weigl *by Kathleen O'Donnell*
Karen Whalley *by Ed Hosselkus*
C.K. Williams *by Catherine Mauger*

AUSABLE PRESS BOARDS & STAFF

With profound thanks for years of generosity and hard work.

Ausable Press is grateful to:

The Council of Literary Magazines and Presses

The New York Community Trust

The New York State Council on the Arts

&
The National Endowment for the Arts

for their generous support.

We are especially grateful to our individual donors, without whom our work would not have been possible.

We participate in the Green Press Initiative. All Ausable books are printed on recycled, acid-free paper.

 **green press**
INITIATIVE